D0402733

VARIETY IN

BIBLICAL PREACHING

Innovative Techniques
and Fresh Forms

HAROLD FREEMAN

VARIETY IN

Innovative Techniques and Fresh Forms

BIBLICAL PREACHING

WITHDRAWN

WORD BOOKS
PUBLISHER
WACO, TEXAS
A DIVISION OF
WORD, INCORPORATED

BV
4211.2
.F74
1987

HIEBERT LIBRARY   38287
Fresno Pacific College - M. B. Seminary
Fresno, Calif. 93702

VARIETY IN BIBLICAL PREACHING

Copyright © 1987 by Harold Freeman.

All rights reserved. No portion of this book may be reproduced
in any form, except for brief quotations in reviews, without
written permission from the publisher.

All the author's quotations of Scripture are from the New
American Standard Bible. © Copyright by the Lockman
Foundation 1960, 1962, 1963, 1968, 1971, 1972, 1973.
Used by permission.

Library of Congress Cataloging in Publication Data

Freeman, Harold, 1936–
  Variety in biblical preaching.

  Bibliography: p.
  Includes index.
  1. Preaching. 2. Bible-Homiletical use. I. Title.
BV4211.2.F74 1987   251   86-26744
ISBN 0-8499-0562-1

7898BKC987654321

Printed in the United States of America

Dedicated to my wife Alice

Contents

Preface

A MAJOR LEAGUE PITCHER who can throw only a good fast ball has too limited a repertoire. If that's all he has, the batter soon learns to anticipate what is coming and hit it. He needs to develop a variety of pitches—a slider, a curve ball, a knuckle ball, a change of pace. The element of surprise will enhance his effectiveness with his standard fast ball. When it comes, it too can surprise the batter.

In the same way, preachers must incorporate a change of pace into their sermonic fare. If they constantly deliver only traditional expository sermons their hearers will learn to anticipate what is coming. If it is a "bad one" they will watch it go by (without comment, hopefully); if it is a "good one" they learn to bat it away with their defense mechanisms and tell us on the way out the door: "That was a good sermon."

This book is offered out of a desire to help preachers find different ways to communicate the old story. It represents a commitment to variety in the form, but constancy in the substance, of biblical preaching. This book was born out of necessity. Some time ago, increasingly interested in teaching students to employ a larger variety in their biblical preaching, I committed myself to teach a new course entitled "Varieties of Biblical Preaching."

Practical considerations made it impossible to deal with all of the nontraditional sermon forms available. I decided to focus intensively on a few and provide an introduction to others. As I began preparing for the course, I found that no single book existed that provided instruction in how to prepare the various sermon models I had in mind. That is the need behind this book. My purpose is to provide in one volume instruction in several nontraditional sermon forms, to furnish the pastor working in the privacy of the church study as well as students in the classroom, with a basic introduction to practical approaches to achieve variety in biblical preaching.

I have made every effort to be practical. Theory is presented first in order to define and validate the various homiletical forms. Suggestions have been added to answer the question of how (the most frequent question surfacing among students in discussions about homiletical innovation). Brief examples are also furnished to clarify the suggestions.

The sermon forms presented are not new. As will be seen in subsequent chapters, some have their roots in models used in biblical times. A few have been used sporadically in the history of the church. All have received attention in homiletical circles prior to this. However, the "trickle-down" from homiletical circles to the functioning preacher has been considerably slow and limited in scope. I hope to accelerate that process.

I am convinced that the approaches here discussed merit a second and closer look. They will, I believe, provide fresh and exciting alternatives as supplements to, not substitutes for, the traditional sermon.

Acknowledgments must be made to others who have provided indispensable assistance. Some of my colleagues in homiletics—Clyde Fant, Jesse Northcutt, Scott Tatum, and Al Fasol—read the entire manuscript and made valuable suggestions, most of which have been incorporated. One problem with teaching preaching is that it assumes a good deal of knowledge about the other theological disciplines. Others have helped with that. Ralph Smith, Dan Kent, and Harry Hunt graciously helped in the area of Old Testament studies. Bruce Corley and Lorin Cranford have provided consultation in New Testament studies. Yandall Woodfin provided help from the perspective of philosophy of religion. Melissa Walker and Janet Wilson very patiently and efficiently provided secretarial and editorial assistance. Gratitude is expressed to one of my student assistants, Bruce Baker, for his help with word processing.

The problem in Jesus' day was that men tended to put the "new wine into old wineskins" (Matt. 9:17). The communication of the Word of God today faces a different challenge. The gospel now sounds like "old wine" to many people. They have heard it all before. The problem, however, is not in the old gospel. Age doesn't hurt wine; it mellows wine. We do not need a "new wine," a new message, but it may be time to put the old wine in new wineskins. It is time for variety in biblical preaching.

Harold Freeman
Southwestern Baptist Theological Seminary
Fort Worth, Texas

Part One

FIRST THINGS FIRST

1

Something Old, Something New

"HERE WE SEEM to be trying to patch up an old form instead of moving into new forms." The setting and substance of that statement provide an accurate overview of the contemporary state of preaching in America.

It came during the National Ecumenical Scriptural-Theological Symposium on Preaching in 1982. The very fact of the meeting indicates the renewed interest in preaching that has occurred during the past few years. In the sixties, preaching in the church was shelved in the interest of the church's activism and social involvement. But the "stubborn pulpit," as Clyde Fant calls it, stayed until its time came around again. It emerged as a dominant feature of church life in the seventies and early eighties.

The substance of the above statement points to two noticeable trends within current homiletics: an adamant reversionism, reemphasizing traditional preaching forms, being countered by an impatient revisionism, experimenting with new models of preaching.

The "old form" referred to the symposium's focus on the homily, a traditional form of Christian sermon. This is symptomatic of one major direction the new interest in preaching is taking. A strong call for a return to biblical preaching in its traditional forms is heard. The expository sermon, for example, is making a comeback. This is easily seen in the themes of various conferences on preaching, the titles of recent publications, and articles in many periodicals.

"New forms" alluded to recent attempts to devise fresh approaches to preaching. The negative comment made by the participant bears witness to the fact that some preachers are restless about a return to the traditional forms. The respondent at the symposium was not alone. Others agreed that an "approach-as-usual" from the pulpit would not work in the new age of the church. They would concur with Clyde Reid that "it is now time to recognize that the old preaching pattern is a yesterday-structure."[1] Many such people, while wanting to participate and contribute to the resurgence of preaching, resist efforts to return to tradition and have opted for novel forms of preaching. Not wanting to be cooks using the old recipes, they prefer instead to experiment with new ingredients, to send up feasts for parishioners with good taste.

Contemporary homiletics consists of these two emphases—a reversion to traditional expository preaching and a revision toward sermonic innovation. Too often these two have gone in entirely different directions. Too much contemporary expository preaching has failed to be creative, and too much contemporary innovative preaching has failed to be biblical. We need to be faithful both to the Bible and our times. This requires that homiletical innovation be wed with exegetical accuracy and hermeneutical responsibility.

Variety doesn't need to *displace* tradition; it couldn't if it wanted to. Traditional approaches have the advantage of years of entrenchment and practical establishment. Probably nothing will ever replace the stand-up monological presentation of an expository sermon as the basic form of biblical preaching. Elizabeth Achtemeier was right:

> Before we discuss these various forms of experimental preaching, . . . let it be said very clearly: There is no substitute for the traditional preaching ministry of the church. . . . There is, by the providence of God, no tool more effective for creating and sustaining the life of the people of God than a well-delivered, well-shaped, proclamational sermon from a well-exegeted biblical text.[2]

Although variety does not need to *displace* tradition, it can *augment* tradition. Several considerations indicate that.

Variety in the Bible

The biblical material itself suggests the need for homiletical variety. Both the varied forms of preaching recorded in the Bible and the varied types of biblical literature legitimize homiletical variation.

Variety of Sermons in the Bible

The Bible contains a record of an interesting assortment of sermon forms. It is noteworthy that instances can be found in Scripture in which spokesmen for God used novel devices analogous to the three main sermon forms presented in this book.

The dramatic monologue message possesses qualities similar to some of the prophets' symbolic acts which they sometimes used to reinforce their spoken words, and sometimes used instead of an oral prophecy. Ezekiel constructed a model of a city under siege (Ezek. 4:1–3); he lay on his side for days signifying being "weighted down" by sin (4:4–8); he cut his hair and beard with a razor and proceeded to burn some of it, throw some of it to the winds, and cut other parts of it in smaller pieces to symbolize the destruction of Jerusalem (5:1–12); and he dug a tunnel through the city wall and dragged his possessions through it as a symbol of the coming dispersion, while the people looked on in astonishment (12:1-16).

Jeremiah broke clay pots as a symbol of the coming judgment on Jerusalem (Jer. 19, 20) and wore an ox yoke to convey the message that his nation and others should submit to Babylon (27, 28). Isaiah presented himself stripped to a loin cloth like a war prisoner or slave, representing the fact that Egypt would be taken prisoner by Assyria (Isa. 20:1-6).

The dialogical sermon also appears in the Bible. In some instances dialogical techniques were used as rhetorical devices designed to engage the *minds* of the hearers; in other instances the speaker obviously intended to evoke an oral response. John Brokhof observes:

> Although dialogical preaching is presently enjoying a comeback, it is nothing new. The Old Testament prophets used this method of communication. Malachi uses the question and answer technique of dialogue: "Will a man rob God? Yet you are robbing me. But you say, 'How are we robbing thee?' In your tithes and offerings" (Malachi 3:8). Ezekiel has Yahweh say, "Yet the house of Israel says, 'The way of the Lord is not just.' O House of Israel, are my ways not just?" (Ezekiel 18:29). John the Baptist was a dialogical preacher. He senses what his congregation is saying: "Do not presume to say to yourselves, 'We have Abraham as our father,' for I tell you, God is able from these stones to raise up children to Abraham" (Matthew 3:9). Jesus was a master at dialogical teaching and preaching. At Caesarea Philippi a crucial situation presented itself. The time had come for the Disciples to realize that he was the Messiah. He did not make a declarative and authoritative claim. He did not try to persuade the men that he was the Christ. He used the dialogical method of questions: "Who do men say that the Son of Man is?" and "Who do you say that I am?" Repeatedly Jesus answered a question by asking a question. At times he allowed the people

to decide, "Which is easier to say, 'Your sins are forgiven' or to say, 'Rise and walk?'" (Matthew 9:5). Once Jesus asked a lawyer to make up his own mind about the meaning of a teaching. At the close of the Good Samaritan parable, he asked, "Which of these three, *do you think*, proved neighbor to the man who fell among the robbers?" (Luke 10:36).[3]

The narrative sermon resembles the story used by Nathan to confront David with his sin (2 Sam. 12:1–12). The retelling of a biblical narrative is prevalent in the preaching of Stephen (Acts 7:2–53) and Paul (Acts 13:16–41); and the parable, often used by Jesus, was a narratively structured device.

An examination of different types of preaching recorded in the Bible then validates the use of various methods, some of which are remarkably similar to the innovative methods of the present time, for communicating the Word of God.

Variety of Literature in the Bible

In addition, the different types of literature found in the Bible call for variation of homiletical forms. Scripture is comprised of legal, historical, narrative, poetic, didactic, dramatic, prophetic, and apocalyptic literature; yet, sermons tend to take on the same form regardless of the form of the biblical literature of the text. Fant describes the production process for most sermons:

For many preachers, unfortunately, seminary training in preaching merely furnished them with a set of homiletical cookie-cutters which they routinely mash down upon the dough of the text, and presto! out pops a little star, or a tree, or a gingerbread man (a five pointed sermon? an organic sermon? a life-situation sermon?). No matter that the text doesn't want to go into these forms; the poor thing is mashed and tortured until it is made to say the things it never intended to say.[4]

The forms traditionally taught and practiced in homiletics have been derived largely from rhetorical theory in Greek and western society. In light of the fact that the biblical literature originated in a non-western Hebraic context, a natural question arises. Why force all of the diverse types of biblical literature into one type of sermon form, particularly one alien to the culture which produced Scripture?

Communication Theory

Communication theory also calls for variety. Our hearers need variety. They have invisible earmuffs they put on when they hear the same sound coming their way. Ineffective, worn-out sensors and overused brain receptors fail to pick up the new message. Calluses have formed at the points where they have been hit again and again. The well-worn paths along the routes of their minds are comparable to the ruts in ours. We need to include in our reservoir of sermonic devices enough variation to interject the element of surprise into our preaching ministry. This will often enable us to put in the point and strike home when the hearers are not expecting it and where they have never heard it before.

Our Culture

Doesn't our very culture also call for variety? Great preaching historically has been responsive to the trends of its time. The shape and style of the sermon has been similar to the style of art, architecture, music, and literature of the time.

Our preaching is not done in a vacuum. It is done in a context of swiftly occurring events and trends. As John Killinger pointed out, "two global wars, nuclear fission, cybernetics, Freud, Stravinski, Picasso, moon shots, wonder drugs, organ transplants, Telstar, ethnic revolutions, confrontation politics, the Beatles, nude theater, LSD—

how many light-years are we away from the church that entered this century?"[5] Yet, many sermons still have the sound of the turn of the century (the *last* one, not the *next* one).

In our kind of world, where the dominant characteristic of modern life is not mere change but acceleration of the rate of change, it will serve us well to be flexible. We need to respond to the shifting patterns of our culture, which has experienced a "ferment over form." The music, art, architecture, theater, and other dimensions of contemporary culture have felt no obligation to pour contemporary concepts and feelings into traditional forms. Function has been considered more important than form.

In such a context it should not be surprising that some of our messages "don't work." They weren't designed "to work," to function. They were designed to fit a certain form—whether it worked or not! In light of the character of our culture, we must be open to new methods of communicating the gospel. Failure to do that indicates an insensitivity to what is happening in the real world our hearers live in.

Our Own Needs

We need variety for our own sakes. How many times during sermon preparation have you felt like a mechanic on an assembly line? "Here I am again doing the same old thing I did last week!" That feeling can take the excitement out of preaching and contribute to ministerial burnout. Already enough forces exist in the ministry to cause that. We don't need to create an additional one ourselves. But we do. As we dig more deeply into our ruts we feel a dullness, our hearers sense a sameness, and we know it! The result is deadening. Nothing different ever happens. We don't plan for it to and they don't expect it to.

Probably the most difficult obstacle to achieving variety doesn't lie in our minds. We can learn new sermon shapes and structures as easily as we learned the ones familiar to us now. The problem lies in our *psyches*. We've grown comfortable with doing things as we've always done them. It's easier and faster to stay with the familiar than to reach for something new. Consequently, as Charles Rice says, we stay "so busy dusting plastic flowers that we do not have time to cultivate roses. In preaching, this translates that we get so busy preparing sermons, we do not have time to examine them or seek new forms for them."[6]

We need to shake ourselves free from the familiar sometimes and try something different. Homiletical variety is needed. The nature of the Bible, communication, our culture, and our own personalities indicate that; but something else is needed also.

2

The Essentials of Biblical Preaching

IN ATTEMPTING TO ACHIEVE homiletical variety, some have sacrificed, consciously or unconsciously, *biblical* preaching. Several attempts at experimental preaching available recently in published form hardly resemble a biblical sermon. No biblical content is in the message or, if there is, there is no evidence of careful exegetical and hermeneutical work behind it. Many of the experimental sermons in circulation, according to Achtemeier,

> can be seriously called into question on the basis of their relation to our understanding of the nature of the biblical word. Many such forms of experimental preaching abandon the biblical message altogether and become nothing more than artistic or symbolic performances, open to a wide variety of meaning, or interesting human discussions of a current topic of the day. Because such performances occur at stated times of worship on a Sunday morning, they are not automatically made into sermons nor do they serve as an adequate substitute for the proclamation of the biblical Word. If the church truly believes that our salvation occurs by our participation in Jesus Christ, then the preaching and

liturgical event are going to have to foster that participation, and they can do so only by the presentation of the Word, as that has been handed on to us in the witness of the Holy Scriptures.[7]

The biblical irresponsibility characteristic of some experimental preaching, however, does not nullify the validity of the experimental forms. It simply invalidates those particular efforts. Such a mistake isn't inevitable. We can learn from the mistakes of others.

Biblical preaching is the relating of biblical truth to contemporary life. The *form* in which that occurs is not crucial. The fact that Scripture is related to life is what determines whether biblical preaching occurs. So, the innovative methods can constitute authentic biblical preaching. Any sermon is a biblical sermon if it confronts the hearers with an accurate interpretation of the biblical revelation and its present meaning for their lives. Innovative biblical preaching is theoretically possible. But how can it be achieved?

The commitment to homiletical variety must be matched by a commitment to biblical responsibility. This involves accurate exegesis and responsible hermeneutics. Biblical preaching must deal effectively both with the Bible and life. Innovative biblical preaching, therefore, must be as solidly based on a proper concept of the nature of biblical preaching as traditional expository preaching is.

The Two-Dimensional Nature of Biblical Preaching

If we derive our concept of preaching from the Bible itself, a biblical message has two points of reference: the prior biblical revelation and the present situation. That is the form of preaching that emerged in the synagogue during the intertestamental period. The Israelite people in exile found themselves worshiping corporately on the Sabbath. However, they were without a central dimension of

worship—the sacrificial system. New ingredients were
needed for worship. One possibility lay in the acceptance
of an increasing amount of literature as sacred scripture. A
pattern of worship gradually emerged in which the Law
and the Prophets were both read on the Sabbath day. When
Hebrew ceased to be the commonly spoken language, an
interpretation became necessary as a supplement to the
reading. Although this interpretation could be expanded
into a detailed exposition, it usually assumed the character
of a rather informal lecture. Thus originated the sermon in
the synagogue.

The synagogue sermon, then, had an exegetical element, in which the Scripture was read or something was
said with reference to the scriptural text, and a prophetic
element, in which the relevance of that Scripture for the
current time was explained. It was "customary to expound
the lessons read in the services. In the Jewish church this
developed into a hortatory address, very near to a modern
sermon."[8]

The distinctive concept of the early Christians was faith
in Jesus as the Messiah. They felt no need to change other
dimensions or elements of their worship. Although the
content was new, old forms could be used. So the early
Christian sermon followed the same form as the synagogue
sermon. "The origin of the Christian sermon, like nearly
everything in the early church services, is to be found in
the Synagogue."[9]

This can be seen by a quick glance at the New Testament
record of the earliest Christian sermons. Jesus went into
his hometown synagogue at Nazareth, opened the scroll of
the prophet Isaiah, read from it, and said: "Today this
Scripture has been fulfilled in your hearing" (Luke 4:21).
Similarly, in the sermon on the day of Pentecost, Peter
observed what was happening and said: "This is what was
spoken of through the prophet" (Acts 2:16). Then he

quoted from the prophecy of Joel. He was interpreting the
current event in light of the prior Scripture. The pattern
repeated itself on Paul's missionary journeys. His pattern
was first to go into the synagogue to preach, hoping there
to find Jewish people ready to accept Jesus as the culmina-
tion of the Old Testament prophecy. So it isn't unusual to
read the sermon in the synagogue at Antioch of Pisidia
(Acts 13:14–41) and find Paul referring to the history of
Israel recorded in the Old Testament writings and then
addressing the present situation of his hearers in light of
his references to their Scripture.

The pattern, then, for biblical preaching appears clearly
in the pages of the Bible itself. The picture emerges of a
two-dimensional nature of biblical preaching. Biblical
preaching has, on the one side, a reference point in the
prior biblical revelation. It has, on the other side, a reference point in the present situation of the hearer. The
preacher works "between two worlds," and a truly biblical
sermon "bridges the gulf between the biblical and modern
worlds, and must be equally earthed in both."[10] Biblical
preaching is pictured in this diagram:

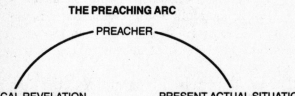

THE PREACHING ARC

PREACHER

PRIOR BIBLICAL REVELATION   PRESENT ACTUAL SITUATION

Biblical preaching, then, is achieved when the preacher
effectively fuses together the prior biblical revelation and
the hearer's present situation, thereby constructing "the
preaching arc." No particular form is required in order for
that to happen. All that is required is that the sermon
function in these two areas. It must deal with the "then of
the text" and "the now of our time."

Touching Both Sides

You create the biblical sermon by the use of two major components: biblically related material and life-related material. These are the functional elements of the message, the way the message works.

The following chapters contain suggestions concerning how to achieve these functional elements in each of the sermon forms. At this point, a larger issue is at hand—whether, and to what extent, these elements are required in a biblical message.

Biblically Related Material

As noted earlier, not all contemporary preaching gives prominence to biblical material. William Toohey painted a picture of a preacher who during the '60s moved in circles where innovative preaching was done. For some reason he had chosen to "go with the Bible" in a particular message. Realizing that this would seem strange to the hearers, he mused about his plans to use the Bible in the upcoming sermon:

> You feel you should say something like, "Tonight, now, try to go along with this. I am not going to read Joan Baez or Dan Berrigan. I just intend to read the Scripture. Will that be alright—just an exception; would that be okay tonight?"[11]

Since that era, both preaching and the Bible have made a comeback, but the integration of the two hasn't always occurred, especially where the person in the pulpit is engaged in the newer forms of preaching. Any kind of apologetic attitude about the Bible must be disposed of. If the experimental sermon is to be a biblical sermon, it must keep in touch with Scripture.

Life-Related Material

While the place of biblically oriented material in the experimental sermon is a question for some, the place and type of life-related material pose questions for others. Some suggest a severe abbreviation or entire elimination of explicit application material in the sermon.

At this point two areas of research in persuasive communication theory relate to our discussion. We need to examine both.

The first focuses on the relative effectiveness of implicit and explicit conclusion-drawing by the speaker. One trend in oral communication theory asserts that in persuasive communication "indirect suggestion is more effective than direct"[12] and that persuasive communication theory should take its cue from the perspective of the "nondirective school of psychotherapy that decisions are more effective when reached independently by the client than when suggested by the therapist."[13]

The second focuses on the relative effectiveness of indirect (overheard) and direct (heard) listening. This approach suggests that a model of persuasive communication be used that somehow creates a situation resembling a hearer "overhearing" (accidentally) rather than "hearing" (directly) the message. It is usually assumed that overhearing is more persuasive because the listeners don't have their defenses built up, are excited about hearing something they shouldn't hear, and don't believe the speaker is trying to influence them.

Pursuing this concept, researchers conducted experiments with groups of Stanford University students. A situation was created in which two people were talking, explicitly agreeing about a subject. Some participants listened in on the conversation, believing that those talking were unaware that they were being heard. Others listened in on the same conversation but were told that those talking were aware that they were listening. Then questionnaires were distributed to both groups of listeners. The result was that those who were in the position of apparently overhearing the conversation indicated a larger change toward the position being advocated in the conversation than those who were aware that the speakers knew they were listening.[14]

The interest in implicit vs. explicit and indirect vs. direct approaches in contemporary persuasive communication theory has caught the attention of homileticians. Some have issued a call for preaching to be less explicit and more indirect. The idea is to have less confrontation by the preacher, allowing more psychological participation by the hearer. At times the suggestion takes the form that sermons should be structured in an indirect mode in which speakers don't address the listeners with direct application of the message. Instead, as Fred Craddock says, the preacher should construct the sermon in such a way that the hearer will be "overhearing the gospel." At other times the suggestion is made that implicit rather than explicit application is better because, as Carl Larson stated in an issue of *Preaching*,

> individuals are becoming more and more reluctant to accept that kind of [explicit] application, religious or otherwise, to their daily lives. That kind of prescription implies that one person is in a position to tell others just what they should do with their daily lives.[15]

In summary, this approach suggests that the preacher should build the application implicitly into the message, allowing the hearers to deal with the subtleties of the sermon and infer the relevant truths of the message for themselves.

However, not all studies demonstrate that indirect, overheard communication is more effective than direct. It should be noted that the experiment mentioned above was performed with Stanford University students as the subjects. That leaves open the question of the relative effectiveness of the two methods of communication when dealing with a heterogeneous group with widely varied intelligence quotients. It is also *very* significant that the researchers acknowledged that an analysis of the constituency of the overhearing group revealed that those who were influenced by what they overheard were already predisposed to believe what they were hearing. The conversation advocated "a position they would like to accept."[16]

Likewise, serious questions are raised concerning the effectiveness of implicit communication that depends on the hearer to draw the intended conclusion. In one experiment

> one of the important messages to be transmitted was "never explicitly stated . . . and it was hoped that the lesson would be inferred by the audience. . . ." They [the researchers] report that the implicit message influenced the more intelligent members but not the less intelligent members of the audience. They concluded: "By virtue of their implicit form, such messages may well have been actually inaccessible to this less intelligent group."[17]

Other experiments raised questions whether it is only the less intelligent who have problems inferring implicit conclusions embedded within indirect communication. A significant experiment was conducted among another group of students, two-thirds of whom were above the national average of intelligence for college students. The project was designed to analyze the relative effectiveness of the explicit and implicit conclusion-drawing. Two types of communication, identical in every way except that in one the communicator drew the conclusion at the end while in the other it was left to the audience, were devised. All subjects heard the identical communication, but for half of them the conclusion-drawing was omitted.

Comparison of the two versions reveals a "very large difference in favor of conclusion-drawing by the communicator. Over twice as many subjects changed their opinions in the direction advocated by the communicator when the conclusion was explicitly drawn than when left to the audience."[18]

Critical of the procedures and interpretation of this experiment, another research group suggested that explicit communication might be *more* effective in bringing about better *comprehension* by the hearer of the speaker's intended conclusion, but *less* effective in bringing about an *attitude change* toward the speaker's point of view. The theory was that intelligent hearers might feel that explicit conclusion-drawing by the speaker is condescending and is an insult to their intelligence. The group designed a new experiment to test the hypothesis that if the hearers of both an explicit and implicit message *understand* the speaker's intended conclusion equally well, more will agree with the speaker's conclusion if he allows them to draw the conclusion for themselves. The results demonstrated that the explicit conclusion-drawing produced better comprehension of the intended conclusion of the speaker and did not adversely affect attitude or acceptance by the hearers. The findings of this study indicate that explicit communication does not necessarily create a negative, "boomerang" backlash among the intelligent hearers.[19]

More recently, an experiment conducted with fifty-two college students, predominantly upperclassmen, yielded similar results. "The speech with the explicit conclusion elicited significantly more attitude change than the speech with the implicit conclusion."[20] Consistent with the results of such research, Bert Bradley in his recent textbook on communication asserts that an explicit statement of purpose by the speaker "aids in changing attitudes of . . . listeners . . . , does not alienate those opposed to the purpose . . . , [and] is . . . more effective with the less intelligent members of an audience."[21]

But let's put research and theory aside for just a moment

and listen to Arthur R. Riel, professor of English at Fairfield University:

> I remember one Trinity Sunday: the preacher was giving us an academic talk on the Trinity. Good! But the dedicated Catholic mother can't help thinking, "This is good, but I gotta get dinner; I hope he doesn't go on too long." Perhaps the preacher should have realized that this thought would be in the minds of his listeners; and anticipating that response, he could have told us all that as we go into the kitchen or as I go to my desk to grade a set of boring papers, the Holy Trinity goes with us. What a thrilling bit of truth. But I never hear it, I have to tell myself about it, and I'm lucky I can. But still I forget; I often need reminders.[22]

These studies and this comment apparently indicate a preference for direct communication in many cases if you intend for the listener to arrive at the same conclusion or application you have in mind.

Faced with some research data supporting implicit, indirect communication and some supporting explicit, direct communication, how do you decide what to do? Perhaps the only valid conclusion is that you will have to arrive at your own choice in the matter. The ball is in your court.

Your own approach to hermeneutics becomes involved at this point. If your approach to the question of the relevance of Scripture for life is primarily from the perspective of the "new hermeneutic," then you may be content to present the biblical material, allowing the sacral Word to create a "language event" that will convey its own meaning while you depend on the Spirit to make it relevant to each hearer. In such an approach, a preacher is not primarily concerned with a historical exegesis and the historical content of the Scripture; rather the preacher presents the biblical material as "call," "demand," or "promise," allowing it to "address," "confront," and "examine" each listener. Pragmatically, this may produce an "impressionistic" approach to preaching, with the hearers free to be impressed with whatever meaning their hearing of the sermon brings to them subjectively.[23]

It is impossible to escape the vulnerability to subjectivism inherent within such indirect communication. Erwin P. Bettinghaus, a highly respected authority in communication theory, addressed that issue by saying, "One of the major barriers to successful persuasion comes with a failure to elicit a response from another individual equivalent to the one intended. In other words, the receiver may not have the same meaning for the term used in a message as did the source."[24]

If, on the other hand, your approach to hermeneutics involves discovering through exegesis and interpretation what the Scripture in its canonical setting[25] *meant* primarily and what *that* means in today's setting, then the question is, Will implicit or explicit conclusion-drawing and application better convey to my hearers the definite meaning I want to convey?

The crucial question for us is, What are the implications for preaching of the experimental research in the theory of persuasive communication? Aware of these studies and responding to this question, Lee Williams, a professor in the field of speech communication and an active Christian layman familiar with Christian preaching, notes that the experiments we have been considering dealt with the matter of conclusion-drawing by the speaker and cautions that

> there is a difference, . . . between explicitly stating your position in the conclusion and telling the audience how to apply that point of view. I feel that it is appropriate to extend these research findings to a sermon situation and say the speaker who explicitly states what he feels the scriptures say (i.e. the "position" the pastor is taking) will be more effective than if he uses an implicit conclusion. However, I do not feel the empirical research . . . can be used to make any judgment about the effectiveness of "explicit

sermon application" (i.e. telling the audience how they can apply the principles established in the sermon). The experimental research was not designed to address the question of application.[26]

He personally advocates that a preacher's statement of a "position" about the meaning of Scripture "should be explicit in almost all cases . . . stating how the audience might apply the message in their own lives . . . might be implicit or explicit, depending on a variety of contingency factors."

Craddock, the most notable advocate of the use of indirect methodology in preaching, acknowledges it is not to be used exclusively, but along with more explicit approaches.[27] For that reason suggestions will be made in the following chapters concerning various available techniques for both approaches. The question still remains concerning how to decide which method to use. Three factors may influence your decision.[28]

The nature of the communicator is one factor. If the hearers trust the communicator, they are more likely to accept the speaker's direct conclusions. If the communicator is suspect, they will not.

The nature of the audience is another consideration. Levels of intelligence and sophistication may indicate the hearers' ability to deal with subtleties. Personality orientation may be significant also. Some people are highly suggestible while others are highly resistant to the suggestions of others.

The nature of the subject under discussion may need to be considered. The familiarity of the subject to the hearer is a clue. A subject with which the hearers are already familiar and with which they are in general agreement might call for an indirect method.[29] The research experimentation cited above seems to indicate that, although indirect communication may not be very effective in *changing* opinion, it may be helpful in *strengthening* opinion already held by the hearers. The complexity of the subject provides another clue. A complex idea with many ramifications or qualifications may prove too difficult for subtlety.

Whether achieved implicitly or explicitly, application must be achieved. Given the two-dimensional nature of biblical preaching, David James Randolph was right. The sermon, he said, should

> intend that the biblical text come to expression in the lives of the hearers. This is not just an addendum to the sermon; it is part of the sermon *by definition* [italics his].
>
> Where concretion is lacking we do not merely find a poor sermon; we find no sermon at all.[30]

Perhaps a responsible and realistic approach would be to attempt to convey, whether by implicit or explicit technique, the meaning of the text in its canonical setting and then suggest various points of the relevance of that for your hearers. At the same time realize that they may infer various points of relevance of the text for themselves. For example, if the true point of the parable of the prodigal son is that God is a "waiting Father," as Helmut Thielicke has pointed out, hopefully, any hearer of a sermon on that parable who is alienated from God would be motivated toward reconciliation with God. Other fall-out applications of the parable might be identified and appropriated by your hearers. A father might realize that he needs to be a loving, waiting, and hoping father toward his own prodigal child. A modern prodigal might realize that he has God-like parents and be motivated toward reconciliation with them. A jealous sibling might realize that intrafamily rivalry should be resolved.

If our innovative preaching is to be biblical preaching, it must touch both sides of the preaching arc: the prior biblical revelation and the present situation. It must speak about the text accurately, and it must speak to life perceptively. But that is not all. It must do both responsibly. And that requires careful movement between the two sides.

3

Managing the Middle

AT THIS POINT WE ARRIVE at what Rudolph Bohren called "the crisis of preaching." What he had reference to is the challenge of fusing together responsibly the prior biblical revelation and the present situation. Too often "somewhere between the text and the sermon an accident takes place. There is a great gulf fixed between the text from the past and the sermon for tomorrow, and no one can jump across it."[31]

The "Dilemma of the Middle"

Bohren calls that gap "the dilemma between text and sermon." One horn of the dilemma is "the tendency to absolutize history." This is the approach of preachers who carefully isolate the text from the larger Christian theological framework, exegete with exacting detail the grammar and syntax of the text, reconstruct the historical setting and meaning of the text, and relay that to the congregation. Having exposed the historical particulars of the text, they fail to go on to any meaningful interpretation of the relevance of the text for their congregations. The sermon actually is oral exegesis, as if the historical and linguistic dimensions of the text were the crux of the sermon. Having answered the question, What *did* it mean? they feel no need to tell what its relevance is.

The other horn of the dilemma is "the tendency to abstract from history through existential interpretation."[32] This is exhibited in preachers whose sermons interpret the text existentially with no connection to the critical, historical, and exegetical study of the text. Such an approach assumes that "after the text has been buried by historical criticism, it is to be brought to life by existential interpretation."[33]

> The method seems merely to be revealing its own schizophrenia: on the one hand it alienates the past through historical criticism; on the other hand it dissolves the past through existential interpretation. It succeeds in utilizing precisely what it denies: a double sense of scripture, the literal (to be grasped through historical criticism) and the mystical (to be gained through existential interpretation).[34]

So, it seems, either way preachers go they are hooked on the horns of the dilemma. They either absolutize the canonical meaning of the text or abstract its contemporary meaning from its canonical meaning.

This whole question of "the dilemma of the middle" presents a greater challenge in the innovative forms of biblical preaching than in the traditional ones. In dramatic monologue and narrative messages, which focus on biblical material, the tendency will be to become impaled on the pole of the biblical revelation and get bogged down in the minutiae of etymologies, historical reconstructions of the textual situation, etc. On the other hand, in the dialogical message, with its strong orientation to the congregation, there will be a tendency to become impaled on the pole of the present situation, stuck with contemporary problems and having no biblical answers with which to get off the hook. On the one hand, the message may never get to life, and it will remain an exercise in critical exegesis.

On the other hand, it may never get to the Bible, and the message will remain a rootless dialogue between preacher and people. Neither is biblical preaching.

Escaping the Dilemma

It is possible to avoid the dilemma. A true dilemma exists, according to *Webster's Third New International Dictionary*, when "a choice or situation (exists) between equally unsatisfactory alternatives." In reality this is not the case with the preacher. One is not faced with a choice of either reciting textual facts or simply reflecting on life. Another possibility presents itself—the possibility of proceeding *through* the middle in a way that will do justice to the integrity of both the prior biblical revelation and the hearers' present situation. The task is to discover the canonical meaning of the text and to discern the meaning of that for the present. The challenge is to negotiate the passage *between* the prior biblical revelation and the hearers' present situation, thus escaping the dilemma.

Although it greatly oversimplifies the problem, the following diagram will help identify and place in proper relationship to one another some concepts that will assist you with the difficulty of managing the middle, between the Bible and life.

	ETERNALIZE "What in this text is *always* true?"	*CONTEMPORIZE* "What in this text is true *now*?"	
TEXT	*UNIVERSALIZE* "What in this text is true for *all people*?"	*PERSONALIZE* "What in this text is true for *you*?"	**SERMON**
	PRINCIPLIZE "Is there a principle behind the particular statement of the text?" (may need to be done)	*PARTICULARIZE* "How does this principle apply to particular situations now?" (suggestive, not prescriptive)	

The steps required to manage the middle responsibly are: *Eternalize* the text by asking, What in this text is always true? *Universalize* the text by asking, What in this text is true for all people? *Principlize* the text by asking, Is there a principle behind the particular statement within this text? With reference to the last of these, many times the biblical statement will be a culturally conditioned particularization—provided for the people, time, and place of the textual situation—of a general principle. In that event, you would need to strip the text of its cultural specifics in order to get at the principle behind it.

Having completed this first part of the process, you're on the move from the prior biblical revelation to the present situation. But you are not there yet. You are now in the realm of abstract ideas. These don't communicate well. So, as a correlation to each of the steps on the textual side of the message, you now take steps toward the "life side" of the message. *Contemporize* the text by pointing out the ideas in it that are true now. *Personalize* the text by underscoring what within it is true for the hearer. *Particularize* the message by suggesting specific ways in which your hearers may apply and implement the principle within the text.

A word needs to be said about both "principlizing" and "particularizing." Here we enter hazardous waters, and caution is in order. With reference to "principlizing," discernment is needed. "Principlizing" may or may *not* need to occur. In some biblical statements you are already looking at the principle. A couple of suggestions may help identify such situations. First, if you find essentially the same thing being said in different strata of biblical literature covering different time frames and different historical situations, the very fact that what is said has been constant probably indicates that it is a principle. It is a constant that has survived all the variables. In this case you don't need to "principlize" the text.

Second, if your exegesis of the text sheds some light on
why the particular statement may have been made to the
people at one time and place, you may well be looking at a
particularization of a larger principle for that environment.
For example, the injunction of the Apostle Paul to the
Corinthian women that they should not cut their hair (1
Cor. 11:6) can be understood as a specific application by
him to them of a larger principle. A study of the situation
in Corinth indicates that women who served as priestesses
in the nearby temple to the goddess of love practiced temple prostitution as an act of worship. The way they were
identified was by the way they cut their hair. Obviously,
then, behind the particular statement to the Corinthian
women asking them not to cut their hair was a larger principle—namely, that Christians should not dress or act in
such a way as to be identified with an anti-Christian life-
style.

With reference to "particularizing," discretion is in order. While you do have biblical authority for enunciating
the principle, you do not have the same level of authority
for dictating to your hearers exactly *how* they must implement that principle in their own lives. It is at that point that
the priesthood of each believer comes into play and the
hearer participates in the message. You may be tempted to
dogmatize and pontificate your own cultural mores with
the same sound of authority with which you articulate the
biblical principle. But you must avoid that. Be suggestive,
not prescriptive.

At this point, response must be made to Ernest Best's
criticism of the concept of what our present discussion has
called "universalizing." He warns against using a process
of "universalization" of a text as the means for building
the bridge between the text and the sermon. He remon-
strates: "If one concrete situation can be universalized
into a desired conclusion, it is almost always possible to

take another concrete situation and universalize it into a directly opposite conclusion. It is the process of universalization which is dangerous."[35] He proceeds to demonstrate what he perceives as a deficiency in the approach by citing sermons by F. W. Robertson and Harry Emerson Fosdick which went astray by using the method of universalizing a text.

A close examination of each of the sermons will reveal, however, that the fault did not lie with the process of universalizing. The problem was a deficiency in exegesis by failing to identify the focal point of the text. The result was the elevation to a universal status of something that was merely incidental, contextual, or situational rather than central and eternal in the text.

The universalizing concept advocated in this book implies accurate stripping of the peripheral matters from the text and preservation of general principles or eternal truths found in it. Surely there are some general, timeless truths that can be inferred from revelation, whether viewed as eventful or propositional (after all, a major school of contemporary philosophy of language insists that language is an "event") at the canonical level and can be verified as authentic by consistency with the entire biblical revelation and correspondence with the revelation in Christ.

The interpretive process suggested in the prior diagram is compatible with any hermeneutical approach that takes seriously the two-dimensional nature of biblical preaching and is committed to maintaining the integral relationship between the meanings of Scripture in its canonical setting and in the contemporary setting. Careful use of this process, combined with responsible, sound exegesis and hermeneutics, will enable you to bridge the gap between the text and the sermon.

You can meet the need for homiletical variety and biblical responsibility. You will need to demonstrate a commitment to achieve creativity, exegetical accuracy, and hermeneutical responsibility. Such commitment will cause you to "touch both sides," to deal with the Bible and life. You can do that responsibly by managing the middle with careful thought processes. From this basis, you are ready to work toward variety in biblical preaching.

PART TWO

THE DRAMATIC MONOLOGUE
MESSAGE

4

Why Does It Work?

THE DRAMATIC MONOLOGUE message is one of the more popular of the contemporary, innovative sermon forms. It uses the technique of presenting biblical truth from the perspective of either a biblical character or an eyewitness of an event recorded in the Bible. The preacher assumes the role of the biblical character speaking directly to the congregation, so this is frequently referred to as "first-person preaching." This form of message offers several advantages and is effective for numerous reasons.

People's Interest in People

This message form capitalizes on people's interest in other people, a fact that is documented by the remarkable success of *People* magazine, one of the biggest profit centers in the Time, Inc., magazine group. *People* is considered a modern-day miracle. Whereas *Sports Illustrated*, published by the same company, was awash in red ink for ten years before turning the corner of profitability, *People* became profitable midway in its second year, 1975. The circulation since 1974 has advanced from 1 million to 2.45 million. At the time of this writing it is the third most widely read weekly magazine in the United States. What explains the success of this publication? One of the editors explains: "*People* was formulated on the premise that the mass audience in 1974 had grown tired of issues and causes. . . . It was time for people to be interested in individual lives again."[1] Many newspapers have followed that lead and now carry a syndicated "People" column. Surveys indicate that such a column is one of the more frequently read sections of the newspaper.

It is simply human nature to be interested in human beings. We identify with other people. The dramatic monologue message capitalizes on that trait, catching the listener up into the message by capturing the hearer's interest in the biblical character.

The Drama of Life

Also, this message form seizes upon people's identity with drama. Our own lives are dramatic, in the sense that dimensions of drama are structured into our existence. Comedy and tragedy are what we feel and experience. Event, happening—these are the stuff of which life is made. Consequently, a biblical message with dramatic dimensions structured into it draws the hearers into the message.

Drama in the Bible

The dramatic monologue can help recapture the excitement originally associated with the biblical revelation. The narratives about the mighty acts of God for Israel must have been stirring when they were passed from generation to generation. The story of the "event" of Jesus was surely electrifying when the good news was told. Reducing these to writing involved a high risk. Papyrus and paper cannot evoke mood and feeling as well as speech can. Centuries of copying, analysis, criticism, and theological systematizing have produced a feeling that the Bible is a collection of ideas. As a result, Killinger said, the church "has largely lost its sense of drama." How unfortunate! I agree with Dorothy Sayers who said, "The Christian faith is the most exciting drama that ever staggered the imagination of man."[2] A message form designed to allow a congregation to share the drama of a personal experience of a biblical character can excite the church again.

Persuasive Communication Theory

In the monologue the preacher can utilize the insights of recent emphases in communication theory. People are bombarded in this media age, not only with words designed to communicate facts, but with visual imagery on the screen. These are augmented by auditory techniques involving both verbal and nonverbal sounds. We experience a "wraparound" communication system.[3] Delivering a sermon in the first person can communicate in this "holistic" way better than an oratorical or declamatory pronouncement of abstract truth. It allows the hearer to feel what the communicator feels, which is one secret of effective, persuasive communication. The crucial question in persuasive communication is well phrased in a country and western song that depicts an older, established country music singer interviewing an aspiring young performer. "Can you make people feel what you feel inside?" he asks.

The dramatic monologue message allows that. It uses the strong appeal of a personal testimony and the emotive qualities of a moving experience. Typically, traditional sermons have an abstract quality to them. The preacher talks about a topic, perhaps "The Forgiveness of Sin." But it is a different thing to listen to someone say from personal experience, "God forgave me." The abstract becomes concrete. The impersonal becomes personal. Cognitive knowledge becomes affective knowledge. The hearer not only *knows* something, but *feels* and *does* something. After all, isn't that the objective of the message?

Connecting Theology and Life

Too often the person listening to a traditional sermon wonders whether or how the truths being articulated by the preacher have any connection with real life. The vague abstractions and generalizations seem far removed from daily reality. On the other hand, people who have long been familiar with biblical stories have never grasped the theological truths embedded in the lives and events recorded in the Bible. The biblical narratives are simple stories which are interesting, but in themselves they may not reveal any substantive ideas. Either way, the Bible is separated from life. The dramatic monologue can overcome that. In it theology is packaged and delivered in the lives of interesting people.

The Bible Comes Alive!

For too many people, the Bible is a book "out of this world," or at least "out of our time." It is about people and things long ago and far away. Naturally people feel that way; they have heard the stories many times since childhood. Having heard them in the same time frame of their lives in which they heard fairy tales, for them somehow the biblical characters seem lost in a netherworld of unreality. Preachers have not always helped the matter. Too much preaching, according to McEachern, seems to be "back there, embalmed in ancient history. The preacher often fails to bring the Bible characters and their life situation into the twentieth century. Thus the sermon seems a futile foray in the dusty trash heaps of some long forgotten civilization."[4]

How tragic when the biblical characters are made to seem unreal. Eric Hoffer, the longshoreman-philosopher, describes his unexpected excitement spawned by his encounter with biblical characters:

The truth . . . of Old Testament history is a palpitating body. All persons, whether heroes or lesser men, are of flesh and blood, real, human, so that after more than two thousand years they seem nearer and more familiar than the personages of our own history, even Washington and Lincoln.[5]

The dramatic monologue message can help resurrect biblical characters from the distant past and from the dusty pages of the Bible and make of them real, live people for the hearers. The biblical character "becomes a personality with vitality instead of just a person-on-the-page in the Bible."[6]

The Hearers See Themselves

This message form, if structured for indirect application, can provide a more effective way of persuading some hearers to apply biblical truth personally. This can be true whether the objective of the sermon is to confront or, on the other hand, to encourage.

Sometimes the preacher's purpose is to challenge the hearer to change a bad life-style. In the traditional sermon the preacher frequently uses a confrontational approach. The hearers are told that they are like some flawed biblical character and they are challenged to change. In the dramatic monologue sermon, the method is involvement and identification. The hearers are allowed to see for themselves the flaws in the biblical character and to realize for themselves that they are like that person and need to change. The approach is based on the idea that

human nature is essentially the same today as it was in biblical times. Some of the characters of the Old and New Testament walk our streets today in modern dress, their temperaments and their basic problems the same as our own. Persons like Judas are sticky-fingered treasurers. . . . Cain still stalks modern parks and alleys. . . . Prejudice did not die with Simon Peter at Caesarea. Salome dances atop the French Quarter bars, and Potiphar is preppy. Canaanite fertility cults are practiced by pill-liberated suburban housewives.[7]

The dramatic monologue message presents the biblical character in a way designed to let the hearers confront themselves as if in a mirror. It not only allows the preacher to get inside the biblical personality; at the same time, it allows the hearer to identify with the biblical character. It is more of a soft sell rather than a hard sell. This is particularly effective for some people who have built up resistance over the years from the recurring confrontations by preachers using hard-hitting sermons.

The hearer's self-identification with the biblical character is a good device also when the purpose is to encourage or affirm the hearer. Most people believe that they are not as good as the men and women in the Bible. They see them as superhuman. But the dramatic monologue message can poignantly depict the biblical characters as struggling human beings wrestling with the harsh realities of life before victory came and before they went down in biblical history as "saints." The hearers can then identify with the characters' humanity and begin to feel hopeful for their own lives and victories.

5

Lay the Groundwork

THE DRAMATIC MONOLOGUE MESSAGE is so different from the kind of sermon we normally write that it may be difficult at first. Several specific suggestions should help.

Select an Objective

At the outset, you need to do for this form of sermon something you should already be doing for every sermon. Determine the objective for the message. Answer the question, What do I want to happen in the lives of my hearers because they have heard this message? Too much preaching accomplishes precisely nothing because we have no precise objective in mind for the message. We may have vague hopes that it will accomplish something, but we have no specific idea as to what that might be. Consequently, our hearers are left hanging, not knowing how to respond even if they feel they should. Every message needs to have a very specific objective. The dramatic monologue message is no exception. The objective will serve three very important functions.

1. *Helps the selective process.* It will work as a guiding principle in the process of selecting the biblical material to

be used in the message. If the central character in the message is a person about whom much is written in various places in the Bible, you may often find yourself aimlessly wandering from one episode of that person's life to another unless something unifies your efforts. Identifying your objective can provide that unifying factor and it will provide clues concerning which events in the person's life to include and which to leave out. This will enable you to cut away the underbrush and stay on the track toward your goal. When you are dealing with a prominent biblical character, McEachern correctly cautions:

> You can't have the character relate all the facts you know about him in one sermon. Choose only the most important facts which relate to your theme. Severe and intelligent pruning will make for a more effective sermon. . . . This principle of limitation of material is important.[8]

2. *Provides focus.* The objective will give you clues concerning particular angles of the biblical incidents or particular dimensions of the character's personality that should be highlighted or amplified. Not all the angles of an event or dimensions of a personality are germane to your purpose in reciting the event or reconstructing the character.

3. *Guides the application.* The intended result will serve to help you apply the monologue. You will know that you need to apply the message at the point of the specific objective, and you will look for the most appropriate way to do that. Application is a challenge in this form of message, as we shall see, and you need all the guidance you can get.

Identify the Biblical Character

After determining the objective of your message, you will need to identify which biblical character will serve your purposes best as the focal character of the monologue. It might be best not to stop with your first impression. Less prominent biblical characters that would serve your purpose more pointedly than the one that first comes to mind may be tucked away in some out-of-the-way place in the Bible. Of course, these two steps can be reversed. You could decide first to preach on a certain biblical character, then identify what objective you want to have for your sermon based on that personality.

Having identified the central character of the message, your next step is research. Achtemeier notices that several dramatic monologue messages in print display a tendency to

> substitute the subjectivity of first-person sermons for hard study of the biblical record. . . . It *is* difficult to research the concrete details of the historical situation of Peter or Paul or some other biblical character, and then to use those as the details of the sermon. But only if such research is done should a first-person sermon be attempted.[9]

Research the Character

Don't depend only upon your memory of the person which may have been formed (or misinformed) from your childhood days in Sunday School. Know the person thoroughly. Explore all the material you can find.

Consult articles about the person in Bible encyclopedias and dictionaries. Through this means, develop as comprehensive a conception of the person as possible. The more facts you know about him or her, the more insight you are likely to have into his or her personality.

Follow the leads in the articles and in concordances to the various Scripture passages dealing with the personality. After reading those Scriptures, study the commentaries on them to gain insight into what each particular citation yields concerning the personality you are studying. By this means you will gain additional insight into various dimensions of the person's character exhibited in different situations.

Biographical studies will prove helpful. Biographical

sermons about the character should yield helpful perspectives.[10] In addition, several books are available which provide excellent information and character sketches of various biblical characters. The well-researched works of Elie Wiesel, Frederick Buechner, Everett F. Harrison, William Barclay, Edith Deen, and Adin Steinsaltz are representative of such responsibly done and richly resourceful books.[11]

Another source to explore is historical fiction involving biblical characters by responsible writers like Fulton Oursler, Lloyd C. Douglas, and Frank G. Slaughter.[12] Such authors of historical novels have usually done excellent research into the biblical characters and their times.

As many as possible of these research sources should be consulted. Obviously, it will be necessary to get your head into books. But a word of caution may be needed: As you use such sources, take care to distinguish fact from fiction.

Research the Setting

Investigate the milieu in which some of the incidents you have chosen to focus upon happened. At this point, your research should include, but take you beyond, such sources as Bible encyclopedias and dictionaries. Secular histories of the era, sociological studies about the time, and nonbiblical Jewish or Graeco-Roman literature representative of the time will all be helpful. The historical, geographical, political, or social situations behind the biblical material are often crucial to an understanding of the character you portray and often helpful in your effort to "humanize" the character. The role of such research in the sermon will be illustrated later in the discussion about the biblically related material in the message.

It should be apparent by now that preparing a dramatic monologue message is harder than preparing a traditional sermon. A great deal of research is required. Achtemeier was right in saying that dramatic monologue messages, "unless extremely well-done on the basis of sound historical and exegetical study, . . . [will] inevitably psychologize the text, adding details never meant to be there, and thus introducing elements which alter and misinterpret the biblical passage."[13] If such a malfunction occurs, the sermon may become more autobiographical of the preacher than biographical of the biblical character.

The emphasis on research raises a caution flag about two matters: unbridled imagination and careless anachronism. The dramatic monologue sermon demands a great deal of imagination. But should it run wild? That has frequently happened. Achtemeier's assessment is that "most first-person sermons engage in a subjective interpretation and psychologizing of the biblical text which can stand up to no scholarly critical scrutiny, and one sometimes suspects that the preacher is using his or her imagination as a substitute for careful exegesis."[14] It is best to steer a steady course between turning the imagination loose and reining it in altogether. Some suggestions may help.

First, with regard to factual matters such as geography or historical events, it would be better to make sure that your imagination stays within the boundaries provided by good exegesis and research. If you convey imagined things contrary to the facts as your hearers know them, you will lose some of your listeners. They may try to mentally verify or invalidate something you have said while you go on with your message. One monologue message I read fused into one person the centurion Cornelius of Caesarea, the centurion with the sick servant from Capernaum, and the centurion at the crucifixion. It presented all of these as the same centurion. Such a contradiction of facts recorded in the Bible is likely to confuse the hearers. They will probably be trying to remember whether all of those were really the same person while the preacher tries to finish the message. If and when the hearers conclude that they themselves are right, the preacher's entire message may be discredited in the hearers' minds. It is better to be sure that the material in the message supplied by your imagination is at least consistent with and not contradictory to what the Scripture presents so that there is no "jolt" or incongruity to the hearer and no loss of credibility by the preacher.

It is probably better to use the imagination in such internal matters as empathy, feelings, and moods. It is also quite natural to imagine the characters as "remembering" something recorded in the strata of Scripture representing a time frame prior to the biblical characters' time—things they would have known about because they possessed some of the Old Testament Scriptures or were aware of the oral tradition from a prior time.

Another problem to be avoided in the dramatic monologue message is the anachronism. McEachern reminds you that, when you are throwing yourself back into a prior time, "it is very easy to let untimely references or jargon slip into the narration. . . . [Even] Shakespeare had a clock strike in his play *Julius Caesar* though clocks had not yet been invented." Try to let your research and historical orientation purge such anachronisms from your vocabulary and reservoir of ideas.

A particular form of anachronism to which a preacher is susceptible is the interjection of "systematized" or "confessionalized" theological schemes into particular biblical situations. Remember that these are representative of post-Chalcedonian Christianity and not biblical situations.

Research, then, should not only put you back in the time of the character, but also take you out of your time. It should prevent anachronism.

Design a Structure

The next step is to organize the thoughts into a functional structure. Of course, this will not be the kind of outline that the listener will hear as "first," "second," "third." But, there will need to be some kind of structure, some pattern of flow designed to move the hearer along in the direction of your objective. Several possible structures are available.

1. *The chronological structure.* In this, you simply describe the events you have chosen as they happened in the sequence of the person's life. The advantage of such a structure is that the sermon's movement corresponds to the hearers' memory of the way the character's life unfolded. This can give a familiarity that can provide a level of comfort for the hearer listening to an unfamiliar sermon form. Often, however, the chronological structure does not provide the strongest movement toward the objective and climax of the message.

2. *The psychological structure.* This alternate structure is available to accomplish your purpose in building toward a climax that focuses on your objective. For example, Peter might first be presented as a deeply spiritual, powerful person enjoying the victories of Pentecost in which he played such a significant part. Then, using a flashback technique, you could portray him remembering his strong commitment to Christ on the night before the crucifixion when he said that he would never deny Jesus but would go to prison or die with him. Having then presented him as a man of strong commitment, with an additional flashback you could proceed, letting him share his tendency to crack under pressure. Now he relates how he stood by the fire and denied Jesus. He could be presented in his deeply pensive, penitent spirit, describing the guilt he felt. Then he could be portrayed reflecting on the fact that God used him at Pentecost even in spite of his prior failure. This structure would well fit a dramatic monologue message with an objective of helping the hearers determine to overcome their failures and allow God to use them effectively.

3. *The dramatic structure.* Another approach would be to structure the sermon along lines commonly used in dramatic forms. You could organize your material so as to answer three silent questions you have in your mind. The

drama begins by answering the question, What is going on here? which produces clear statements describing the situation in all its various dimensions. Next, the drama continues by addressing the question, What are the ramifications of this situation? that is, the complications of the situation are portrayed in a way designed to arouse suspense concerning its outcome. At the end the story answers the question, How did this turn out?

6

Plan the Content

THE NEXT STEP is to plan the fleshing out of the structure by providing these: an introduction to the message, biblically related material, life-related material, and, perhaps, illustrative material.

The Introduction of the Message

The introduction to a dramatic monologue message will, of course, need to be different from a typical sermon introduction. You will need to accomplish two things in it—introduce the character and give the sermon's focus. You can introduce the personality of the monologue to the congregation in an introductory moment or two in which you assume your normal pastoral role before taking the role of the biblical character. If you choose this method, you would speak in the third person *about* the character before speaking in the first person *as* the character. In these first remarks, you would set the scene and introduce the character. When you have never attempted this form of message, such a method may provide a degree of comfort for you, and it will not startle your congregation or leave them guessing about what is happening, which would likely be the case should you immediately launch into the monologue.

With some congregations, or after you have introduced this new sermon form to your own people, it may not be necessary to start "out of character." Beginning "in character," you may simply state: "My name is _____ ; I'm from the village of _____ ." You can also do this less abruptly and more creatively and imaginatively by first sharing something about the character with which they are familiar so that they will begin to identify who he or she is. You would need to move rather quickly and smoothly to identify the person specifically so that the congregation will not be left wondering whether they have guessed correctly. For example, "I'm a skeptic by nature. It was never easy for me to believe anything. Even when my friends were totally convinced by something, I doubted it. They came one day telling me they had seen Jesus alive after his crucifixion. I doubted it. My name is Thomas."

A second function of the introduction is to focus on the particular dimension of the character's personality you have chosen, as well as the particular event or events in the person's life, and the objective of your message. If, for example, your objective for the message is to encourage Christians to make a comeback after a failure and you have chosen Simon Peter's comeback as the basis for your message, very early after identifying him you would want to say something like: "I tragically failed Jesus once, but I found out that he gives a second chance. Let me tell you how I know."

Biblically Related Content

You are now ready to provide another element of the sermon, the biblically related material. The exegetical and hermeneutical work necessary becomes more crucial in the dramatic monologue message than for a typical expository sermon for a very practical reason—you are locked out of some types of sermon content. A bulk of application material, which normally consumes a good part of the traditional sermon, is not usable in the monologue. Consequently, the biblically related material will occupy a proportionately larger segment of the message than usual. And since this is so, it may be helpful to suggest several types of biblically related material that is particularly appropriate to this form of message. The following rather extensive list is not intended to suggest that you should use all of them in a single message. Together, these provide a large reservoir of possibilities from which you may draw those particularly suited to the message you are preparing. In any one message, several of these approaches can be used together.

Historical Incident

Retelling the historical incident or incidents around which the message revolves is the most basic method. This is done by simply narrating loosely the appropriate narratives recorded in Scripture. Of course, since it is done in the first person, you will need to avoid a dispassionate recital or mere itemization of the details of the narrative. Instead, you will want to provide a dynamic, vital—even exciting—monologue. You will want to communicate the character of the incident in the same way you would share any exciting event or feeling from your own life.

Historical Framework

It is often helpful to rebuild the historical framework in which the person lived or in which the event occurred.

For example, perhaps your objective for a message is to encourage your hearers to take a stand for God even against enormous odds. Suppose you have chosen to portray Elijah reflecting back upon the confrontation he had with the priests and prophets of Baal on Mount Carmel. Although not all details of the historical setting are contained in the narrative in 1 Kings 18, you can aid your hearers by reconstructing for them the facts concerning the reign of King Ahab in Israel and his marriage to Jezebel, along with the importation of the priests and prophets of Baal.

Historical Locale

Information about the historical locale in which the event occurred or in which the person lived will often prove helpful. Israel is a small country, and many of the different narratives in Scripture have their setting in places that were already of historical interest by the time of the character or event you are portraying. Many events recorded in the New Testament happened in places prominent in Old Testament literature. The use of Bible dictionaries and encyclopedias will help you recognize which prominent biblical events would have occurred already in the location in which your message is set. For example, you could picture blind Bartimaeus in Jericho speculating something like this:

> They tell me that in the old city of Jericho God did something great for my ancestors when they came across the Jordan to inherit this land. As the story goes, by a miracle he knocked down the walls. They tell me that was important because it was the key defense position for the western section of the wide plain of the promised land. It had to be taken if my forebears were to have the promised land. It was the only way they could get into the land. God performed a miracle for them near here—right down the road where the old city of Jericho stood! I wonder if the God who worked so long ago still works today? I wonder whether the God who took care of the masses would do something for just me?

Social Situation

Portraying the social situation behind the text is often very helpful, depending upon the particular subject or personality with which you are dealing. For example, if you are portraying one of the lepers healed by Jesus, it would be helpful to have the character portray the sociological dynamics accompanying leprosy in New Testament times. The lepers were ostracized and, by Levitical law, forced to maintain a prescribed amount of space between themselves and others. This, of course, is not indicated in the biblical narrative telling of the healing of the leper. It is discovered either from commentaries' observations about the story recorded in the Gospel or by studying the subject of leprosy in Bible encyclopedias and dictionaries. A good grasp of the sociological ramifications surrounding an event will help "humanize" the story and provide appropriate pathos in the message.

Geography and Topography

Describing the geographical and topographical setting of the place will often provide helpful perspective and sensory appeal. These factors can enable you to provide your hearers a vivid description of the surroundings in which the event happened or in which the character found himself.

You could, for example, when portraying Peter in Galilee, describe Mount Hermon with its snowcapped peaks visible to the north of the Sea of Galilee on a clear day. When depicting Paul in prison at Caesarea, portray him as looking westward toward Rome and seeing the red reflection of the setting sun on the blue Mediterranean. The physical features discovered about a place can easily be used even though they may not be mentioned in the Scripture with which you are dealing.

Another example: the text that narrates the story of the healing of blind Bartimaeus says nothing about sycamore trees; but the text tells us that it happened in Jericho, and you know from something else that happened in Jericho, the encounter Jesus had with Zaccheus, that sycamore trees were common there. So, in describing Bartimaeus's situation you could easily portray him saying: "I sit here daily against the trunk of this sycamore tree begging because I am blind."

Political Situation

Information about the political situation behind the Scripture often is necessary in order to get a point across. Peter can serve as an example again. If you are portraying his dilemma between loyalty to Jesus and his instincts for survival at the time of the crucifixion, it would be necessary to clarify for the hearers how the Roman presence in Jerusalem impacted decisions about death sentences. The fact that the native civil and religious authorities no longer had power of capital punishment, which was reserved for the representative of Rome, would be important to understand why Jesus was shuttled back and forth between Caiaphas, Herod, and Pilate. It would be helpful, too, to narrate how Pilate happened to be in Jerusalem for the festival of the Feast of the Passover even though the procurator of Judea normally lived in Caesarea.

Personal Characteristics

Pointing out some of the characteristics of the people involved in the Scriptures you are dealing with can often be very helpful. You will, of course, need to reflect your character's own characteristics, which you will have learned from your study of Scripture. Be sure to glean this material from the broad range of Scripture, as well as from a study of the particular text(s) of focus. If the central character was involved with other personalities of the incident, it would be helpful to reconstruct their characteristics also.

Sensory Dimensions

Reproducing the sensory dimensions of the text is vital. Utilizing as many of the five senses as possible, describe the time, the place, and the people. Help your hearers hear the winds howling through the valley toward the Sea of Galilee. Help them see the deep blue waters of Galilee nestled 700 feet below sea level between the rolling mountains to the north and the craggy cliffs to the east. Help them sense the smell of fish around the sea and feel the dust on the disciples' sandals.

Empathy with the Character

Creating the probable *mood*, *feelings*, and *emotions* of the personality should be a very strong ingredient in such a message. Empathize with the character. This is what will make the story become the *human* story—the drama of life. The things that people identify with are the *human* things—warm handshakes, a good night's sleep, a recovery from sickness, an amply laid table, a well-watered earth. For example, if you portray a leper, help your hearers feel the effects of the social isolation of leprosy by saying: "As if it were not enough to have this disease—I have to endure it alone. I can't even touch my child. I can't even go home."

These are some ways in which you can deal with the biblical material in writing the dramatic monologue message. These are not the only ways, but they are representative. Reading them probably has caused you to be aware of other ways of digging into the Scripture and its background in order to supply material for your message.

Application Content

Another basic component in a biblical message is the application of the truth to the lives of your hearers. Achieving this is a particular challenge in the dramatic monologue message. However, given the two-dimensional definition of biblical preaching, it must be done. No one seriously questions whether the hearer should get the point of the message. The only question is how to make that happen in a dramatic monologue message. In the light of the discussion in chapter 1 about the relative merits of direct and indirect application, suggestions follow for achieving this dimension of the message by either method.

Direct Application

Knowing your congregation and yourself, you may feel that explicit, direct application is in order. This can be achieved in more than one way.

1. *Change character*. It's possible, of course, to step out of character at the end of the monologue, assume your pastoral role, and press the point of the message to your hearers. James Flamming constructed a message revolving around Cornelius in this way. Toward the end of the message, he portrayed Cornelius in the house where Simon Peter shared the gospel with him. He ended the message with a concluding statement from "Cornelius" followed by a direct application by "the preacher." In written form below, the change of paragraphs represents the change of speakers. When delivered, a break in the vocal pattern would be necessary in order for the hearer to discern the difference.

All of God's great joy and presence came right down into that room. Tears started coming down my cheeks, and I knew I had found it—the meaning and the purpose of everything I had always hoped and looked for. A Gentile. A soldier. Now a follower. How about you, have you found what you are looking for?

Would you bow your heads? Stand with me, reverently, very quietly. I step now out of the shoes of Cornelius, back into the shoes of the pastor of this congregation, and I ask you, have you found what you are looking for? Has Jesus Christ become personally yours? Are you one of his sons or daughters? Has his living Spirit so entered your life? If not, why not this day? For I have told you a true story of a man who found God. And would you, with him this morning say, "I want him, I want him?"[15]

This method of applying the message will be most comfortable to some. But it has potentially schizophrenic qualities. If the last words of the character have been well chosen, the sermon reaches a poignant climax in the conclusion of the monologue. It can be anticlimactic for the dramatic effect to be lost in the transition back into the character of the preacher.

2. *Let someone help you.* An alternate form of direct application that would not require that you break character is possible. In this method, you would stay in character and fade off the scene into the wings. At that point, someone else—either another minister or a layperson who is comfortable with public speaking—could apply the sermon to the hearers. You would work with that person in advance, helping prepare the application. Although this method doesn't require the character to be broken, it still requires that the mood be broken; and that can be a liability.

3. *A soliloquy is possible.* Some may prefer a method that still provides direct application while allowing the character and mood to be preserved. Some can do this rather effectively by following the pattern of the Shakespearean soliloquy where Mark Antony stays in character but addresses the audience about what is happening on the stage. By the very nature of the dramatic monologue message, your character has already come through a time tunnel and is speaking directly to the congregation. You could simply stay in character and speak directly to your hearers about the relevance of the message for their lives. Ray Burchette chose this method for a sermon revolving around the character of Simon Peter. Reflecting on the days spent with Jesus after the resurrection and before the ascension, he said:

Oh, many wonderful things happened over the next few days. He met several of us at the sea. He fixed breakfast for us. He told me to feed his sheep. Those were great days.

But of all I shall never forget—one thing stands clearest—forgiveness. I had failed him not once, not twice—but numerous times. I had bragged of how I would stand by him, and I had crumbled like a weak rock. But Jesus refused to allow that failure to be the final word in my life. Forgiveness was offered and was accepted. Sure there are times when my failures seek to haunt me. There are times when they try to rule me—but I refuse to allow it. For I have known God's mercy. I have experienced his forgiveness and a new beginning. That is the truth about me.

And you—what of you? Are you allowing some failure to be all that is said of you? Don't do that. There is forgiveness just for the taking. There's a wideness in God's mercy—accept it—now![16]

Indirect Application

Some feel that any form of direct application is inappropriate to a dramatic monologue message. McEachern suggests that in this form of sermon the "application has to be self-evident or implicit rather than explicit" and that "most hearers are more capable of making their own application than we preachers think."[17]

In order to achieve this type of application, you will need to avoid breaking character. Even while remaining in character, however, you can use alternate tactics to achieve indirect application.

1. *Reflection by the character is a good approach.* Depict the character reflecting upon the truth of his own story and sharing it with the listeners. This strategy calls for the hearer to identify and appropriate the truth about which the character muses. Ernest Campbell used this approach in a sermon about Simon Peter that centered on the Great Confession at Caesarea Philippi. The sermon moved toward a conclusion by depicting Peter reflecting on his statement, "You are the Christ, the Son of the Living God." Then Peter reflects:

I must have said the right thing. Beginner's luck I guess! For no sooner had I finished than a broad smile crossed his face. He sprang to his feet and said with glistening eyes:

"Blessed art thou, Simon, son of John! For flesh and blood has not revealed this to you, but my Father who is in heaven. You are Peter and on this rock I will build my church."

He was as happy as I had ever seen him and his joy was contagious. Presently we were all up giving each other "the peace" and pounding one another's shoulders. We had done something good for him for a change; in some small way had ministered to a need he had to be rightly understood. And to think that what I said would be the rock confession of the church's faith!

Less than a year later my faith lost its anchor and I was adrift on a sea of doubt. The nails that ripped his flesh killed my dreams and crucified my hopes. Where was God when this was going on? What would happen to me? The rock had turned to sand.

Then on a day for which all other days were made I heard the welcome news that Jesus was alive. Nothing was over. Everything had just begun. He was more, not less, than I had hoped. So he would ever be.

. . . How wondrously strange and how much more than coincidence that when I told him who he was I learned who I was too![18]

And so, the point was made that people really find themselves when they find Christ. Here the application is made by the character of the monologue stating an eternal truth designed to be identified, understood, and appropriated by the hearer.

2. *Constructing a conversation is a creative approach.* Portray the character as if he were speaking to an imagined person of his own time. Frederick Speakman put the congregation in a situation of "overhearing" the character discuss the truths of his life with someone else. In this

particular message the Bethlehem innkeeper speaks to Luke, who has come years later to do research in preparation for writing his Gospel. In the quotation below, the change of paragraphs indicates the move toward indirect application. It portrays the innkeeper asking a question of Luke and elaborating on its implications.

> The inn was crowded as never before; we had bedding on the roof and even tents pitched in the alleys. And when this fellow of about my age came along that evening imploring us for lodging, he was just another like the many I'd turned away all day.
>
> How are you ever going to know life's moments when they come, Luke? The great hours, the shining hours, the ones that later can mean much—they come walking up looking like any other hour. And always when you're busy. Always when you're so convinced that something else you're doing is so important. And you let them go on and never know. I think that has gnawed me the rawest—that I'd have sent that couple away.[19]

Here the innkeeper is placed in the role of asking common human questions that were as characteristic of life then as they are now. As the hearers listen in on the innkeeper asking those questions, they hopefully will understand that they also have moments in life that are significant, moments they are all too prone to pass by. No overt attempt is made by the preacher to communicate that explicitly.

These represent several ways in which the sermon can be applied. It will not be easy. The preacher will find it challenging, but it must be done if the attempt is to become a dramatic monologue message instead of just a drama.

Illustration Content

Although biblically related material will comprise the majority of the message and life-related material (application) will supply some portion, there are other typical components of a biblical sermon that can be utilized. Illustration, for example, can be provided.

On the surface, it might appear that no illustrative factor is needed because one of the functions of illustration—the creation of interest—is already provided automatically in this message form by its very life and vitality. However, an illustrative dimension can clarify and reinforce crucial parts of the message.

At first it might seem as if there were no way to use illustrations in the monologue sermon. It might seem difficult, since you are locked into playing that character, to do anything more than simply reconstruct his or her personality, situation, and environment. That isn't true, however. Such an impression probably arises from too narrow a concept of illustration, consisting for the most part of secondhand stories we have heard or read about. That is not the best kind of illustrative material, anyway. Working with a broader range of illustrative material, you can find ways to provide illustration in the dramatic monologue message.

Analogical Illustrations

One of the most effective kinds of illustrative material is the use of analogy, in which spiritual truths are compared to commonplace events or circumstances in order to clarify and reinforce truth. You probably create analogies often in your sermon work. This device can also be used in the dramatic monologue. Put yourself back into the character's place. Let him or her observe nature, society, or people that comprised the milieu of that time; then portray him or her drawing analogies between the things observed and the thoughts being expressed.

Biblical Illustrations

The Hebrew people of all Old Testament periods were intensely aware of their heritage. Many characters representing the later biblical periods, having access to sacred writings or oral tradition, would easily have known about the prominent characters of an earlier era. Jeremiah, for example, was almost certainly influenced by Hosea. Beyond the awareness of historical figures preceding them, some Old Testament personalities likely knew and interacted with other Old Testament personalities of the same period. It may well be, for example, that Amos influenced Hosea, his contemporary. In such cases an Old Testament character could use another Old Testament character as an illustration.

In addition to the availability of Old Testament narratives, some New Testament events or characters would be available for use as illustrative material, depending on the character you are portraying. The time factor in the writing of the New Testament (the simple fact that the Gospels narrate incidents that occurred during some three or three and one-half years, but the entire New Testament literature reflects developments during decades following that) indicates that biblical characters representing a later time in the New Testament era could easily be portrayed as looking back upon people, situations, and incidents prior to their own time about which they would have known. They might have known of these because they were referred to in documents such as a "sayings source" or "early Gospel" already in circulation in their time and later used as sources by the authors of the Gospels as we now have them (although the existence of *Q* and *Ur-Marcus* is now contested).

Beyond the written sources, oral tradition about many of the New Testament characters and events already was being created and preserved. Hearsay would have made it possible for one New Testament character to have known about another. For example, since Bartimaeus was healed of his blindness just outside Jericho (Luke 18), Zaccheus (Luke 19) could easily be pictured as thinking about what he heard Jesus had done for Bartimaeus and wondering whether Jesus cared as much for tax collectors as he did for blind men.

Current Events Then

You can portray characters referring to events of their own time to illustrate what they are saying. Events recorded in both secular and sacred literature of the time might easily have been known by the character you are portraying. For example, if you are representing Peter restlessly wandering around Caiaphas' courtyard while Jesus is being interrogated, you could convey his struggle and indecision by saying something like this:

> If this thing ends up in Pilate's court, that could be real trouble. He doesn't mind bloodletting. I remember hearing about the time when he mingled the blood of the Galileans with their sacrifices (cf. Luke 13:1).

In this case, the knowledge of the event about which the character is thinking has come to us by the biblical record. However, it would be possible also to refer to events mentioned, not in Scripture but in secular literature about the times. Some noncanonical Jewish and Graeco-Roman writings reflect the history and happenings of that time. Bible encyclopedias and dictionary articles about prominent biblical characters often serve as good secondary sources, because they treat in some detail such events. Such research would enable you to present Peter as saying:

> Pilate crushes his opposition. Just across the valley, up on the Temple mount, he sent his soldiers into the Temple Treasury to take money to finance an aqueduct. When my Jewish brothers rioted, he sent his troops in with staves and swords.[20]

Current Events Now

You could portray the character as aware of some common, generally known situation in our time. The very situation of picturing the characters as coming from eternity through a time tunnel into our time would imply their familiarity with "where we are." The "good Samaritan," for example, could illustrate the Jewish-Samaritan prejudice by saying, "It was like your black-white prejudices." The widow who gave all she had could illustrate her commitment by saying, "It was like your endorsing your social security check over to the church when that's the only income you have."

The use of illustrative material presents a real challenge in the dramatic monologue message. However, creative preachers will find that they are able to incorporate the illustrative factor in the message.

7

Writing and Delivering the Message

HAVING PLANNED the type of content you need for the biblically related, life-related, and illustrative material of the message you are now ready to write the message.

Writing the Manuscript

You will probably find it helpful to write a full manuscript for the dramatic monologue message, even though this may not be your normal method of sermon preparation. Without that, there will be a tendency during the presentation to wander around rather than to move in a straight line toward your objective. You may end up giving too much historical or biographical information about the biblical personality and lose sight of the purpose of the message. Full manuscript preparation does have a potential liability—the delivery of the sermon could sound more like a recitation of a manuscript than a shared story. But that can be avoided if you deliver the message correctly.

As you write the manuscript, consider the audience. The sermon must be related to needs or situations in their lives. They must be able to identify with the character.

Don't stay in historical minutiae to the exclusion of the human interest angles of the story or the timeless truths that are trapped within that incident. Consider the dramatic qualities of suspense, emotion, movement, conflict, and decision.

Be sure to write the manuscript in conversational style. This, of course, is the proper style for any message, but it becomes particularly crucial in the dramatic monologue message. Since the person who is the focus of the message will be presented as talking naturally, anything that tends toward abstract, literary style would ruin the effect of the sermon. The sermon will need to be informal and conversational in tone.

To facilitate that, familiarize yourself with the style used in contemporary fiction. George Bernard Shaw said: "The task of the novice is to acquire the literary skill; the challenge of the adept is to get rid of it." Contemporary writers have risen to that challenge, and your production of a manuscript for the dramatic monologue message will need to follow their patterns.

Specific suggestions may be helpful. Use short sentences. Use sentence fragments when they would occur in normal conversation. Allow the sentence structure to reflect the informality of conversation. Use short, simple verbs. Place the verbs in the active voice. Use contractions when they would be used in normal conversation. Favor specific words over general, abstract ones. Employ concrete nouns and personal pronouns.

If you need help acquiring the skill of writing with oral style, refer to one of several good sources on the subject.[21] The most practical help, however, is a simple procedure: say it aloud before you write it. Normally in writing we move from thought to paper (or word processor). Try something new. Interject a step between the thought and the paper—say it aloud. Then write what you say. That will insure natural, oral style.

Preparing to Deliver
the Message

The purpose of writing the manuscript is not to provide you something to memorize, but to force yourself to think through the message carefully. Not many could memorize the sermon. Even if you succeeded, that could affect adversely the delivery. The result would probably sound more like an oration than a conversation. It probably would be better to follow the advice of W. E. Sangster to "think paragraphically," memorizing the *key segments* on which the message revolves and thoroughly familiarizing yourself with the other paragraphs.

A significant part of your personal preparation is "getting into character" and into the mood of the situation. I use the phrase "getting into character" with some reservation. It's possible that, with some people, this will lead to "overkill and acting."[22] To prevent that, you may need to employ an alternate technique discussed later concerning "The Narrative Message" (see page 159). In either technique, imagine yourself in the situation of the character, and let your feelings emerge.

Oral preparation will be very helpful. Vocalize the message a number of times in privacy, noticing whether the sound of your voice is compatible with the content of what is being said at each point along the way. Using a recorder-playback machine may be helpful at this point.

Normal questions arise concerning any necessary logistical preparations that might be peculiar to the dramatic monologue. It is possible to use several theatrical aids to enhance the presentation. Such things as lighting effects, costumes, and props can be used. In many churches the financial and human resources are available to do that. Where these things can be utilized well, they may be desirable. However, all of that is not necessary and may come across as too theatrical. If the content of the monologue is good, if the delivery is natural, and if you are comfortable in normal clothing, the presentation can be very effective this way. Getting into character is much more important than getting into costume.

Delivering the Message

Because this sermonic form is very different from the typical sermon, you might first get comfortable with it and help your congregation to become familiar with it by presenting a monologue message written by someone else. It should, of course, be acknowledged to the congregation that you are doing this. With that experience behind you, if you choose, it will be time to deliver your own monologue.

Having earlier underscored the importance of conversational style in *writing* the message, it's now time to emphasize the importance of it in the *delivery*. One of my earliest experiences with a student attempting a dramatic monologue message found him saying, "I am Joseph, the carpenter, the father of Jesus" with the same tone and volume in which a fervent revivalist preacher would say, "You'll go to hell if you don't trust Jesus!" After the opening line it was downhill the rest of the way. Anything smacking of a "preachery" style or "ministerial tone" will negate the effect of the sermon. Remember, you are a person talking, not a preacher preaching. During the oral presentation, you will need to take extra care to use the vocal variables of volume, the rate of your speech, and the pitch of your voice in such a way as to reproduce normal conversational style.

Body language, also, is important. Few people naturally talk in informal situations with the stilted, restrained posture used by many behind the pulpit. Be very much aware of the thoughts and feelings that would normally be present in the life of the character you are portraying. Make sure your use of facial expression, posture, and movement of hands and body are naturally expressive of the thoughts and moods you are communicating through words. Here Craddock's advice is very helpful. Allow the eyes to "move about in the same general direction as the tongue."[23] For example, when the content of the message moves toward the character's reflections or reveries, you will want to look off in the distance in a pensive way rather than confront the congregation with the strong eye contact usually associated with the more traditional, direct approach. Since body language is particularly crucial to the dramatic monologue, you may find it helpful to remove the pulpit, leaving yourself entirely visible and open to the congregation. Unlocking yourself from the pulpit may free you up. After all, very few of the biblical characters had one! Its presence between you and the people will obstruct their perceiving you as the biblical character as well as inhibit your body language.

Some last words about the monologue may be helpful. You may think that a preacher with an introspective or introverted personality (and, by the way, most of my students every year categorize themselves that way) could not do the dramatic monologue message because it would require an actor. Actually, however, it may be true that preachers who are more inclined toward the sedate, deliberate delivery style will experience an unusual freedom of personality while delivering the dramatic monologue message. They may be able, under the umbrella of assuming another personality, to act like that person would without worrying about how atypical their demeanor is for their own personalities. It was either James Stewart or Henry Fonda, both of whom are known to have been personally shy, who reminisced on his acting experience and said: "The truth is that it is real therapy for a self-conscious man. You put on a mask. You are no longer yourself; therefore you are free to act like someone else."

Use the dramatic monologue with an awareness of its inherent pitfalls, one of which is the danger of being too theatrical. You are primarily a preacher, not an actor. You're delivering a message, not a performance. It is easy also for the sermon to slip over into the fantastic and sensational and fail to do justice either to the biblical material or to the nature of preaching. Good, careful exegesis enlivened with intellectual honesty and prayerful imagination will help avoid this problem.

You will find that the monologue is not an easy method of preaching. It takes more work than the traditional sermon, but used properly it can produce gratifying results. It will be a fresh experience for your hearers, and it can put a new enthusiasm in your preaching by challenging you with a new method.

Few things are more helpful than examples or models. For that reason the excerpts from several dramatic monologue messages never published or in books now out of print have been included as examples earlier in this chapter. The additional study of examples of dramatic monologue preaching currently available in published form will prove helpful.[24]

Part Three

THE DIALOGICAL MESSAGE

8

Reviving an Old Form

As POINTED OUT EARLIER, a dialogical dimension has deep roots in early Christian preaching. But somewhere along the way, the development of a professional clergy and the formalization of worship submerged the dialogical dimension of preaching.[1] It came to the point that "the preacher does the sermon."

In 1928 Sinclair Lewis wrote his book *Elmer Gantry*, depicting his concept of the typical preacher. The fictional Gantry lived in a midwestern community and went off to a small Baptist college. Under the strong influence of some religious students and pious faculty members he "got saved." Several noticed his impressive physical appearance and charismatic personality and knew those were the makings of a fine preacher. They shared with him their vision of him as a great "man of God" and he "got called to preach." Soon after he had accepted the call, he was assigned to preach. It was a struggle, but he came through and preached his first sermon. Afterward, he began to contend with the "temptations" of smoking and drinking, and he liked the vices so much that he began to wonder whether he was really called to preach or had been persuaded to enter the ministry by some very shrewd people. He began to think about other vocations. But, he reflected on that one experience of preaching and said:

> Yes, sir! The whole crowd! Turned to me like I was an All-American preacher!
> Wouldn't be so bad to be a preacher if you had a big church and—Lot easier than digging out law-cases and having to put it over a jury and another lawyer smart'n you are.
> The crowd have to swallow what you tell 'em in a pulpit, and no back-talk or cross examination allowed.[2]

For some, things haven't changed in the fifty years since the book was published. Unfortunately, the Elmer Gantry character isn't dead. Some preachers still think of preaching exclusively as a "you sit still and listen while I tell you something" situation.

Contemporary Cultural Considerations

However, things *have* changed and the preacher will do well to be aware of the changes. Great preaching has always been a result of interaction with, rather than isolation from, the trends of the times. Some significant factors in our present situation indicate a need for an increased dialogical dimension in preaching.

Contemporary Communication Theory

Historically, communication theory hasn't emphasized the dialogical dimension. What's going on by the speaker has been considered more important than what's going on in the hearer. Consequently, rhetoric, a set of guidelines for the speaker, has been the focus of attention.

Experimental work in the field of communication theory following World War II contributed toward a concept of communication as basically dialogical. It is now recognized that persuasive communication must sometimes be a two-way street. Bettinghaus points out the opinion of many that the traditional model

> is no longer adequate. We must extend persuasive communication beyond this simple model. Because we live in a pluralistic society, because we are so highly interdependent, the *cooperation* of all participants in this society is required if we are to make decisions and keep the society moving. . . . It is no longer enough to look at persuasion as a one-way street, with the source actively communicating, and a receiver passively receiving.[3]

Philosophical Theological Thought

Another cooperative dynamic that contributes to the concept of communication as basically dialogical is the thought of the Jewish philosopher-theologian Martin Buber. He pointed out that man has a tendency to reduce other people to objects. The ideal, he said, is an "I-Thou" relationship between people. Otherwise, an "I-It" relationship exists, in which one person may have objective knowledge about another person without having real knowledge of the person. He said that we have the alternatives of "the life of dialogue and the life of monologue."[4] Translated into the preaching situation, his insight means that the traditional sermon sounds very much as if preachers are telling the listeners what they know about the subject (it); the need now is for preachers to consider the hearers as persons and talk *with* them rather than *to* them about it. Beyond Buber, the whole existentialist thrust would call for the hearer's involvement during the preaching experience.

Sociological Trends

The recent emergence of the Third World on the international scene is only a symptom of the emergence of the common person in our time. Ours is increasingly a populist age. The common man clamors for a voice. People don't want to be ruled. They want a piece of the action. We deal with a "new situation" with a "new authority structure" and, consequently, a "new communication structure."[5]

Consequently, the church and community no longer automatically accept the preacher as the authority figure. The "prince of the pulpit" has been dethroned, and if he tries to restore the monarchy he'll be defrocked. The emergence of strong lay movements in the church probably has at least as many roots in sociology as in the Bible. The people in church, like people at large, want a piece of the action.

Whether we like it or not, they are talking back. Sometimes they literally talk to us after church, reacting to something we've said. More often than not they talk about us among themselves. And, frequently, the thinking and more sensitive members of the congregation are talking within themselves about what we are saying. It is inherent in the democratic structure of our culture. And yet, tradition holds on:

> Basically, as it is generally practiced, preaching is a monologue by one man directed at his congregation. The listener has no opportunity to express his doubts or disagreements to the assembled group. He may even know factually that the preacher is wrong about some of the statements he makes in his monologue. An authoritarian structure is one in which power is focused in the leader and preaching may be thought of in this sense.[6]

It's time to get in touch with the times and give the people a participative role in preaching.

Technological Developments

Until recently, viewers of the movie or television screen played a passive role, except for the involvement of their emotions. That is beginning to change. The screen is beginning to evoke response. Some television communication techniques now provide devices designed to allow viewer feedback to the studio. Educational television systems provide opportunity for a teacher in one location to hear and respond to questions asked by different groups of viewers in separate locations. Some video display terminals project questions (up to now, primarily yes or no type answers only are possible) for the computer operator to answer by response to the keyboard. Some computers, however, have the capacity for voice-activated response.

What of the future? *U.S. News and World Report* celebrated its fiftieth year of publication with a segment predicting developments in the next fifty years. On the public entertainment front, it suggested that

> on the horizon for Hollywood is the development of experience cinema. . . . Entrepreneurs envision a 360-degree screen that makes members of the audience feel as if they are in the middle of the picture.
>
> Movies of tomorrow may even be participatory films in which members of the audience could select the direction the plot would take by pressing buttons on their chairs.[7]

On the private entertainment side, it suggested that the old family den would be transformed into a media room with 3-D television.

A writer has warned us to think of the possibilities:

> Three-D television will bring culture right into your den. *Three's Company* can become *Four's Company,* if you like. Audience-participation *Hamlet* can be dialed up (you'd best watch yourself during the final scene or you won't be around for the summer reruns).[8]

Developments in our culture are creating dialogical dynamics. Our preaching will be done in a *participative* culture.

Biblical and Theological
Considerations

The participative dimension of preaching is not just a concession to contemporary trends. It is consistent with the Bible and the theology of preaching.

Biblical Examples

Since the background of the Christian sermon lay in the synagogue, the form of the early Christian sermon was a replica of the Jewish sermon in the synagogue. An informality and openness prevailed in the synagogue setting. Notice the account of Jesus speaking in the synagogue at Nazareth. After he stood to read from Isaiah, "He closed the book, and gave it back to the attendant, and sat down; and the eyes of all in the synagogue were fixed upon him. And he began to say to them, 'Today this Scripture has been fulfilled in your hearing'" (Luke 4:20–21). Then the account narrates the following discussion of the people among themselves and their dialogue with him, all of which occurred while they were still "in the synagogue" (v. 28).

Notice, also, the "after-sermon dialogue" between Simon Peter and some of his hearers on the day of Pentecost. Peter ended his sermon by saying: "Therefore let all the house of Israel know for certain that God has made him both Lord and Christ—this Jesus whom you crucified" (Acts 2:36). That was the end of the sermon. Verse 37 continues the narrative: "Now when they heard this, they were pierced to the heart, and said to Peter and the rest of the apostles, 'Brethren, what shall we do?'"

The next verse narrates the response of Simon Peter to their inquiry: "And Peter said to them, 'Repent, and let each of you be baptized in the name of Jesus Christ for the forgiveness of your sins; and you shall receive the gift of the Holy Spirit.'" Here Simon Peter had engaged the minds of his hearers to the point that they had questions they wanted to ask, and he took the opportunity to respond. If, then, we model our preaching after the early church we must, as William Thompson points out, acknowledge "the dialogues in which Jesus was constantly engaged and the early Christian worship in synagogues in which everybody present had his say!"[9] The truth is that we have biblical precedent for dialogical preaching.

Theological Concepts

A proper theology of preaching, worship, and the church calls for involvement by all the people of God. Together these form a strong argument for dialogical preaching.

1. The theology of preaching contains two concepts that validate dialogical preaching. Let's look at both.

a) Preaching is communal. A long time ago P. T. Forsyth advanced the view that "the one great preacher in history . . . is the church. And the first business of the individual preacher is to enable the church to preach."[10] Craddock agrees:

> If the preacher is addressing the church in his sermon, he should recognize them as the people of God and realize that his message is theirs also. He speaks not only to them but for them and seeks to activate their meanings in relation to what he is saying.[11]

b) Preaching is incarnational. Early in the twentieth century Forsyth said that "with preaching Christianity stands or falls because it is the declaration of a gospel. Nay, more—far more—it is the Gospel prolonging and declaring itself."[12] This hinted at a concept of preaching as something more than a human endeavor; it was seen as a divine event. Since that time, numerous theologians have depicted preaching as "existential encounter, a redemptive deed, and a divine act."[13] Donald Miller asserts that to preach the gospel . . . is not merely to say words but to effect a deed. To preach is not merely to stand in a pulpit and speak, no matter how eloquently and how effectively, nor even to set forth a theology, no matter how clearly it is stated nor how worthy the theology. To preach is to become a part of a dynamic event wherein the living, redeeming God reproduces his act of redemption in a living encounter with men through the preacher. True preaching is an extension of the Incarnation into the contemporary moment, the transfiguring of the cross and the resurrection from ancient facts of a remote past into living realities of the present.[14]

John Stott, while admiring such a high view of preaching, has been reluctant to call preaching an "extension of the Incarnation." He raises the question:

In what sense can the herald by his proclamation "prolong" or effect an "extension" or "continuance" of God's redemptive act in the cross? . . .

. . . I believe . . . that it is by preaching that God makes past history a present reality. The cross was, and will always remain, a unique historical event of the past. And there it will remain, in the past, in the books, unless God himself makes it real and relevant to men today. It is by preaching, in which he makes his appeal to men through men, that God accomplishes this miracle. He opens their eyes to see its true meaning, its eternal value and its abiding merit.[15]

Clyde Fant combined the admirably high view of preaching as a divine, redemptive event with a caution apparently designed to reserve a unique place for the historical incarnation in Jesus. He said that

the incarnation . . . is the *truest theological model* [italics mine] for preaching because it was God's ultimate act of communication. Jesus, who was the Christ, most perfectly said God to us because the eternal Word took on human flesh in a contemporary situation. Preaching cannot do otherwise.[16]

This statement seems to preserve the best of both truths: a view of preaching as an event in which God confronts persons by "enfleshing" his Word in a preacher and a view of the historical incarnation in Jesus as unique.

It is important to acknowledge *some* difference between what happened in Bethlehem and what happens in your pulpit on Sunday morning. Is it only a difference of degree? Perhaps it will do justice to both the singularity of the Christ-event and a lofty view of preaching to think of the Incarnation in Jesus as the "once-for-all" norm of the way God becomes involved with us, and of the incarnational dimension of preaching as the contemporary channel through which God's Word really becomes involved functionally with our human speech. Such a concept of preaching perceives of it as personal encounter between God and the hearer. And what does that have to do with dialogical preaching? If, in fact, God speaks to other persons through the person of the preacher, an integral relationship between preacher and people exists which implies the dialogical nature of the sermon.

2. An adequate theology of worship implies an active congregation. The dialogical sermon can foster Kierkegaard's understanding of worship. Drawing an analogy between church and theater, he reversed the traditional concept of the worship situation in which God is seen as the prompter, the preacher is seen as the performer, and the congregation is viewed as the audience. Instead, he suggested that the preacher is prompter, the hearers are the performers, and God is the audience. The congregation, in such a design of worship, is active.[17]

3. An adequate theology of the church emphasizes all of God's people. But the reality of church life hasn't always embodied that idea. Bohren pictured the monopoly the preacher has held on the sermon. He compared the situation in worship to a symphonic and choral presentation in which

the clergyman directs, plays first violin, and sings the solo. At most, the chorus provides a musical background.

. . . The terrible thing is that . . . the laity are allowed only to . . . lay the music on the stands, as it were, and occasionally play the triangle.

There is a picture . . . from top to bottom chairs, music stands, kettledrums, snare drums, violins, violas, flutes; somewhere on a chair a musician, tired, his arms folded; obviously intermission. The picture of our congregation today. It is vital to summon the players, show them their instruments, and give them the pitch.[18]

Together, then, contemporary considerations combined with biblical and theological considerations call for the dialogical dimension of preaching. This can be achieved in two ways. Before discussing them, however, a clarification is needed, and a caution is in order.

First, the clarification. A clear distinction between dialogue as a method and dialogue as a principle will be helpful. Reuel Howe explains:

By *method* we mean the way the communication is delivered: in monologue, for example, one person addresses another; in dialogue two people exchange communication. By *principle* we mean the whole concern that governs the communication; when the monological principle is employed, one person tells another what he ought to know, and the communication is content centered; when the dialogical principle governs a communication, the speaker feels responsible for and responds to the patterns of experience and understanding that his listener brings to the situation, and thus the listener is encouraged to grapple with his own meaning in relation to the speaker's meaning.[19]

This distinction implies that a monological method in preaching may, in spirit and mood, be dialogical. And, conversely, merely using a dialogical method doesn't guarantee *true* dialogue. The ideal is for communication to be dialogical in principle whatever form or method is employed.

Now the caution. Achtemeier is on target, noting that of many recent efforts at dialogical sermons

> most are little more than planned discussions having no relation to the biblical story, and while they may raise issues upon which the congregation may reflect—not a bad goal to be sure!—they are not substitutes for a biblical sermon. If there is to be a dialogue sermon, it should be based on a biblical text.[20]

9

Increasing the Dialogue in Your Preaching

MORE THAN ONE HUNDRED YEARS AGO Schleiermacher sounded the first modern call for the dialogical factor in preaching.[21] In America, fifty years ago, Fosdick called for the abandonment of a monological spirit and the development of a dialogical spirit in the sermon. The preacher, he said, should

> so build his sermon that it will be, not a dogmatic monologue but a co-operative dialogue in which all sorts of things *in the minds* [italics mine] of the congregation—objections, question, doubts, and confirmations—will be brought to the front and fairly dealt with.[22]

Notice, the thrust of his statement calls for a *mental* dialogue, not necessarily an oral dialogue, between the speaker and his hearers.

All preaching should be dialogical in effect. Even in the traditional sermon where one person stands and speaks for twenty minutes, dialogue should occur in the sense that an interaction takes place between the speaker's mind and the hearer's mind. The day is long gone when preaching should be thought of as oration. It should be thought of as communication. You can increase the dialogical effect of a sermon by using certain stylistic techniques. Think of yourself as talking with each person in the congregation. Use rhetorical questions. Anticipate the questions the hearers will have about the sermon and answer them. Anticipate and answer their objections to the message. Use first and second person pronouns ("you" or "we"). Maintain eye contact. Use simple language.[23]

You can go beyond stylistic matters in creating a partnership in preaching between you and your congregation. You can structure a method whereby they share with you the preparation of the message or the implementation of the message. Several possibilities exist.

Presermon "Feed-in Groups"

People tend to participate fully in the things they have an investment in. The dialogical dimension of any form of mon will be enhanced if some members of a congregation have gathered ahead of time to "get on the same track" that the next Sunday's message will be on. Presermon seminars or "feed-in groups"[24] to allow that can prove very helpful. The group could consist of selected or volunteer members of the congregation. Ask them to study the passage of Scripture that will be the focus for the next Sunday's message. Get together with them early in the week. The group can help in the following ways.

1. *Helping with biblical material.* Ask them to help prepare the part of the message containing biblically related material. Ask the question, What do you think this passage of Scripture means? The answers may be accurate. However, many of the answers likely will be incomplete, to say the least, or inaccurate. Normally, laypeople will not have the advantage of working exegetically on the text. So, what good are wrong answers? Hearing their answers will bring insight into the frequent misunderstandings of a given passage of Scripture, enabling you to sharpen your focus on

ways in which the text needs to be explained to the larger congregation. Their answers may indicate the need to focus more clearly on the literary context of the passage, its historical context, or its grammar and syntax. It is better to let several inform you of their conceptions or misconceptions than for you to sit and guess how the text needs to be explained.

2. *Helping with application.* Ask their help with the life-related segments of the sermon. Relevant application is becoming increasingly difficult for any one person to identify. In this "hi-tech" era you probably know very little, if anything, about the workaday world of many of your members. And in an urban setting where a "megachurch" serves large congregations spread out in sprawling suburbs you may know little or nothing about the family life and leisure habits of the members. It is very difficult to sit in a study and identify the various human needs and problems to which a passage of Scripture relates. Why guess? After the group has achieved clarification of the real meaning of the passage, put the question to the laypeople: "What does that truth mean for your life?"

For example, if the truth excavated from the passage is that God is always with his people, the relevance of that truth will take various shapes according to the situations of the hearers. The businessman might sense this means that when the tide is running against him and he is tempted to do something unscrupulous in order to survive, he will be aware of the presence of God in the office or in the corporate board room. A woman competing for a niche in the corporate world or trying to find her place in her own private world might point out that God will be with her at the office or at home. She may tell how knowing of his presence will affect the decisions she makes and the way she spends her time. The widow may feel its primary meaning is that during the long hours, and days and nights of loneliness, she is not alone. A young person might identify the relevance of the presence of God in his or her life in terms of reinforcing his or her commitment to Christian convictions even when such a commitment is not popular at school.

It is possible by imagination to put yourself in your people's shoes. Normally, however, they can tell us a good deal more than we can ever imagine for ourselves. You can incorporate into the message at the appropriate place the applications to your hearers that have previously been identified in the small groups.

Spending time with presermon discussion groups requires the investment of time, but it can yield an increased relevance of the message. It can certainly help bring the sermon into contact with reality, thereby increasing the dialogical principle by helping the preacher preach to where the people are.

Postsermon Feedback Groups

The idea of a group meeting after the service for discussion about the sermon is not all that new, either. Joseph Fort Newton used the after-church talkback sessions more than fifty years ago.[25] Volunteers can be requested, or you may select and invite certain members of the congregation to meet at some time after the sermon to engage in conversation with you about the message.

Begin by inviting them to ask you anything they would like. Suggest that perhaps they didn't agree with a part of the message. Encourage their participation by assuring them that you are open—that no question about the message is off limits.

If the group doesn't begin to dialogue with you, take the initiative by probing: "What did the sermon say to you?" "What difference do you think this sermon should make in your life?" "What did you not understand about the message?"

Interaction centered around these questions will enhance the dialogical principle in the sermon on the next occasion. For one thing, those participating in the talkback sessions will be listening more intently so they can interact more responsibly. Also, however, you will be gaining insights from your people about the way they go about relating Scripture to their lives. Understanding that, you can normally do a more effective job of making messages more relevant to all of your hearers.

All of these devices can help you become more dialogical in the effect of your own preaching. But you can go beyond that.

10

Including Others in a
Dialogical Message

IN THIS APPROACH, "within the context of public worship
. . . two or more persons engage in a verbal exchange as
the sermon or message."[26] In the previous section we have
been dealing with dialogical procedures before or after the
sermon designed to increase the dialogical principle in the
monological method. Now, we are talking about a dialogical methodology for the message itself. This can be
achieved in either of two ways—the pulpit dialogue or the
congregational dialogue.

The Pulpit Dialogue

According to this method, another person (or persons)
joins the preacher on the platform and participates in the
oral presentation of the sermon.[27] According to Killinger,
this can help rescue preaching from seeming like a stellar
performance of a "mere solo act by the senior minister on a
highwire."[28] Several patterns present opportunities.

Some sermons are two-point sermons. The second point
either is a contrast, a corollary, or an extension of the first.
Another minister or a layperson within the church could
present one of these parts of the sermon.

Some Scripture passages focus on a biblical character. After reading the text, you move to the first phase of the message, an introduction in which you present the subject of your message, the background of the text, and the individual around whom the text centers. As this phase draws to a conclusion, the second phase begins with the character approaching the pulpit where you will "interview" him or her. He or she may enter in costume or street clothes, as you prefer. (I have a preference for ordinary clothes, as discussed in the dramatic monologue message.) When the character arrives at the altar area, move from behind the pulpit to meet him or her and proceed with the interview. In the third phase the character exits and you return to the pulpit to draw together the point of the interview. For example, the parable of the prodigal son could be presented by your narrating the story, then looking up to see the central figure of the story coming across the platform. A simple transition will work: "Look, here he comes now. Let's talk to him." Then interview him. Ask probing questions that would allow the returned prodigal to tell about the waste he made of his life and of the waiting father's love. Following this, as the "prodigal" exits, you could drive home the point of the persistent love of the Father.

An adaptation of this would be to use the same format above, introducing the Scripture and character first. But the second step would not be a dialogue. Bring the first part to a close by saying, "But look, here comes Simon Peter now. Let's let *him* tell his *own* story." Then, the second major part of the sermon would be, in effect, a small version of a dramatic monologue, a "minimonologue." In the third component of the sermon, the character exits, leaving you to reflect with the congregation upon what the character has said. At this point, make the message relevant to the lives of the people and the congregation.

Structurally, the above two suggestions take similar forms: In the first, the pattern is (1) introduction, (2) interview,

and (3) interpretation. In the second, the pattern is (1) introduction, (2) minimonologue, and (3) interpretation.

In the role-play message, two or more people are cast in
the role of biblical characters, and they engage in dramatic
conversation. This is particularly adaptable to a text that
contains a comparison or contrast element. For example, in
dealing with the parable of the good Samaritan in Luke
10:25–37, seven persons could be used. Some of them, cast
in the roles of the lawyer and Jesus, could be on one side of
the platform. Others cast in the roles of the priest, the Levite, the Samaritan, and the injured man in the ditch could
be on the other side. At another place, the innkeeper could
be waiting for the Samaritan and the injured man. Each of
them would engage in dialogue, amplifying the conversa-
tions actually recorded in the text. In this case, you would
construct a conversation between Jesus and the lawyer, suc-
cessive minimonologues—conveying the thoughts of the
priest and the Levite—and a conversation between the Samaritan, the Jew, and the innkeeper.

The conversation would reflect their situations and
thoughts consistent with your research of the nature of
priests, Levites, and the Samaritan-Jewish relationship. It
is important in this passage to portray the lawyer and Jesus,
however. Frequently, the parable is presented alone; but,
you should remember that the parable was told by Jesus
within a setting and it would be important to present the
setting. If the sermon is begun with a conversation between the lawyer and Jesus, the sermon could be brought
to a conclusion with an application in which the lawyer
turns to the congregation and puts to them the question he
put to Jesus: "Who is *your* neighbor?" Then the person
representing Jesus could say to the congregation what he
said to the lawyer: "Go thou and do likewise."

In a similar way, for example, Luke 15:11–32 (the parable of the prodigal son) could be presented with a crowd
on stage. They would represent the same people men-

tioned in verse 1 of the chapter, which tells of the publicans and sinners gathering around Jesus, and the Pharisees and scribes reacting to that. On the other side of the stage persons could be cast in the role of the father, the elder son, and the prodigal son. Again, each of them would share conversation consistent with what you would present about the character if you were preaching a well-researched, straight monological sermon about them.

A natural question is, "In what sense does this form of dialogical message differ from the drama?" The essential difference revolves around several factors. Most religious dramatic presentations are not well-researched biblically; the role-play sermons should have as thorough exegesis and research behind them as any sermon.

That leads to a second difference: In drama, imagination is usually unrestrained; in this type of sermon, the imagination is informed by exegesis and restrained to the point of consistency with good exegesis. Third, when done well, no props or theatrics are needed. Most importantly, in this sermon form you communicate and highlight eternal truths and their relevance today at some point along the way. This can be done by incorporating these truths into the dialogue of the characters and highlighting them as the really important thing said. Or, as suggested earlier, it can be done, particularly with reference to the parabolic passages, by having Jesus stand to one side and introduce the drama just as the text records that he introduced the parable. When the drama has ended, he can speak to the congregation just as he would have spoken to his disciples at the conclusion of the parable, applying the lesson of the parable.

These are some ways that dialogical method can be incorporated into the message itself by planning a sermon form that calls for oral participation by two or more people on the platform.

But this does not exhaust the possibilities for the dialogical method in the form of the sermon. Not all the dialogue has to occur in the pulpit.

The Congregational Dialogue

Members of the congregation can interact vocally with the preacher *during* the time of the message, speaking from their places in the congregation or coming to the platform. This is certainly a break from traditional approaches to preaching, in which as Craddock put it, "if the congregation is on the team, it is as javelin catcher."[29] In the traditional monological sermon, the congregation is always on the receiving end. That can be changed. Congregational dialogue is one of the more striking and impressive varieties of preaching. The hearers will certainly recognize it as a new departure. We preachers do too. Who hasn't been afraid that someone in the congregation might stand up and talk back to us during a sermon? At the same time it is probably one of the easier innovations to begin with.

Because vocal participation during the sermon time will be a significant departure from the routine, your congregation may be more comfortable at first knowing that you have control of the situation (not to mention the fact that you may feel more comfortable having control, too!). The use of the "controlled" method can "loosen you and your people up" toward eventual use of a more spontaneous dialogical methodology.

The Controlled Dialogue

You can carefully structure the message in such a way as to assure your control of the unity, direction, and progression of the sermon. Although a condescending posture is inherently built into a controlled dialogue, some of the suggested forms that follow will, I trust, prove less patronizing than others. Several possibilities exist.

1. The *supplemental dialogue sermon* opens up large possibilities for lay participation. It is also a relatively easy

innovative form to implement. I call it the supplemental dialogue because people in the congregation are supplementing the presentation of the sermon by orally supplying various parts of the message.

a) *Supplemental Scripture reading* is the simplest method of introducing dialogical methodology to a congregation. You may be preaching a multitext message, in which two or three points are each related to different passages of Scripture. By prearrangement, at the appropriate places in the sermon, various members of the congregation could be prepared to stand where they are and read the previously assigned Scripture aloud. You can achieve this in a simple fashion by saying: "I have asked _____ to read another passage of Scripture for us." The participants probably will feel more comfortable saying something aloud if they know that you will tell the whole congregation that they have been asked in advance to do it. The shock effect on the congregation also will be lessened by this fact.

b) *Supplemental illustrative material* can be effectively presented by laypeople. This is one of the easiest ways to adopt a dialogical sermon style.

Good illustrative material often comes from fields of inquiry and study in which engineers, scientists, sportsmen, artists, or garden club members in the congregation are more knowledgeable than the preacher. They can do a better job than we can of sharing the particular dimensions of the illustration, and it will come across to the hearers with an authenticity often absent when our congregations hear us speaking authoritatively of matters about which we don't know very much.

Also, incidents, experiences, or situations revolving around people in the congregation can often provide poignant illustrative content. Of course, it is never appropriate to betray a confidence or intrude on privacy. However, occasionally you might feel comfortable asking a person if he or she would be willing to share something personal to illustrate your point. If so, you could arrange for that person to rise and ask, with "apparent spontaneity," "Preacher, could I say a word about that?" Then, let the person tell the story. (Caution: You might not want to use this kind of dialogue with a congregation in which there are numerous people who have wanted to say a lot of things for a long time! They might mistake the apparent spontaneity for the real thing and use the opportunity to get something off their chest.)

For the sake of more comfort, you could remove the apparent spontaneity feature by saying, "Mrs. Smith had an experience like that not too long ago. I've asked her to share it briefly with you." When she has finished speaking, resume by moving to your next point.

You will find that a story told firsthand in the form of a testimony will pack a great deal more punch than will your secondhand telling of it. It's some kind of a commentary on us as preachers that when the laypeople share their own stories a great deal more credibility is usually given to the account.

c) *Supplemental application* can also be presented by a member of the congregation. By sharing with some people ahead of time the basic points of your sermon, you can ask them to be thinking of how a specific point applies to their lives. By prearrangement, instruct them to be ready to stand and speak at the appropriate time about how that truth is applicable to them.

For example, if one of the points of the sermon has to do with honesty, a student could talk about the need for honesty on campus and in the classroom, telling, perhaps, about a situation where he or she was strongly tempted to cheat. A housewife could talk about the need for honesty on her part with the members of her family or honesty as she talks about other people in the community. A businessman could talk about the need for honesty in face of the fact that every businessman knows several ways he could profitably cheat in his business.

2. The pursuit-of-truth sermon offers another possibility. Perhaps you remember a basic sermon outline pattern called the "chase" technique. In this, the sermon is in pursuit of the truth, and it moves along the lines of very natural questions the congregation will have about a given subject. Or, it deals with the possible answers they anticipate when the title of the sermon raises a question. The sermon takes the following shape:

    I. Is it _____ ? No.
   II. Is it _____ ? No.
  III. Is it _____ ? Yes.

In this particular type of sermon development, the possible answers that are wrong are presented first, and the correct answer is presented last. It is possible and easy for this type of sermon to be converted into a congregational dialogue. By prearrangement, you could ask people to stand and ask the questions that are the points of the sermon rather than your articulating the questions as you normally would. For example, you could develop your introduction up to the point at which you are ready to move toward answering the question, How does a person become a Christian? Then, on cue, someone in the congregation could say, "Is it by something the person alone does?" You would then develop your point by answering the question. A second person could then say, on cue, "Well, if it's not just something that a person does, is it something that only God does?" at which point you would reply in the negative with an explanation. Again, on cue a third person could synthesize the two by asking: "Well, then, is there something that God does and people accept?" You then drive the point of the sermon home that salvation comes by God's grace and man's faith response.

It will be necessary for you to plan very carefully the transitional sentences between the points so that those who are participating with you in the congregation will hear the transitional statements and take them as the cues for their questions. Depending on your congregation, before you begin you may feel the need to inform the congregation of what to expect. In that way you will be more assured of keeping them with you when the "surprise" comes.

The Spontaneous Dialogue

I know the obvious opposite to a controlled dialogue is an out-of-control dialogue, but I prefer to call it something else. A spontaneous congregational dialogue offers possibilities weighted with some risk, but it also has the potential of great benefit. You can encourage your congregation to share questions, comments, reaction, and response to a prior sermon. The possibility of this is totally unexpected on the part of the average listener. You may have to go out of your way to let them know that you are inviting them to talk and, in fact, that you expect them to speak to you from where they are in the congregation. You may even have to prime the pump by prompting one or two people ahead of time to start the discussion. Because this is so novel and unexpected, at first it will probably work more readily during a Sunday evening worship time rather than during a Sunday morning service. People are a bit "gun shy." They have been preached *to* so long that they have no idea that there is the possibility that they will preach *with* the preacher.

In my tradition, it is customary for churches to hold Sunday evening worship services. My own experience has been moderately successful in securing spontaneous, unplanned oral response during the evening sermon hour to the question: "Would somebody share a question or a thought you have had about the morning message?" Hopefully, something you say during a sermon will always trigger another thought in the mind of the listener; he or she pursues that thought often while the sermon goes on to other things. This means you have struck a nerve in that listener, and it may well be that if he or she articulates the thought, in response to your question, someone else in the congregation will gain insights about your sermon content or subject that previously had evaded them. So, make the effort with the entire returning group on Sunday night to try to create oral dialogue about the morning message.

A variant form of spontaneous dialogue would involve your presenting only half a sermon—the textually related material, leaving the remainder of the time for your hearers to dialogue with you about its relevance.

> The minister can give a brief exegesis before the discussion begins, to clear away any misunderstanding of the text's historical setting and theological thrust. The task of the congregation is then to apply themselves.[30]

These approaches to dialogical preaching which provide a time for spontaneous congregational participation probably offer the best opportunity for indirect application or implicit conclusion-drawing by the preacher. The open-endedness of the situation leaves opportunity for others to infer the implications and corollaries of what has been said in the sermon and to state them in the hearing of the larger group. Some who would "never have thought of *that*" can be taken by surprise when a fellow member of the congregation articulates the relevance of some part of the sermon. In the process, the less sensitive ones can be made more sensitive to dialoguing with you as you preach. Others may start listening to see what they can get out of the message.

There are, then, many ways to evoke a more participative spirit in preaching. Finding your own way to do it will help make preaching more of an encounter with the Word of God for your hearers. Additional help is available for those who wish to pursue this sermon form further.[31]

Part Four

THE NARRATIVE MESSAGE

11

It All Began with "The Story"

THE SERMON as "story" is the most recent emphasis in preaching. How long it takes to get back to basics!

The Significance of "Story" in the Christian Faith

The bottom line of the Christian faith is a story—the story of God's redemptive activity in the world. It has all of the drama inherent within a story—comedy and tragedy, joy and sorrow.

That primal story of God's redemptive activity gave rise to separate "stories" about how, when, where, and with whom God was doing his work. Those stories are the material of which, to a great extent, Scripture is made. Narrative is a dominant literary form in the Bible.

Regardless of your perspective on dating some of the Old Testament material, the fact is that centuries intervened between the time God began to do his work of redemption through the patriarchs and the time of the writing of the Pentateuchal material recording the stories of their lives. Behind the written narratives of the Old Testament lay the pattern of one generation telling another the stories of Abraham, Isaac, Jacob, and Joseph. The patriarchal narratives were followed by chronicles and histories of the continuing story of God's redemptive activity in Israel.

Stories are not only behind the Old Testament narrative literature; they often lie just beneath the surface of other literary forms in Scripture. They are often in the background of didactic Old Testament literature. G. Ernest Wright pointed out that much Old Testament theology is "recital" theology, "the confessional recital of the redemptive acts of God."[1]

It is much the same with the New Testament. Significant time elapsed between the pivotal events of the New Testament era and the Gospels as we have them. Behind the Gospels lay literary sources upon which the Gospel writers drew; and behind those lay oral tradition. It's obvious that such stories existed from the closing statement of the Gospel of John: "And there are also many other things which Jesus did, which if they were written in detail, I suppose that even the world itself would not contain the books which were written" (John 21:25).

In the New Testament, also, the didactic and epistolary literature grew out of reflection on the implications of the story of God in Christ. The other New Testament literary forms were intended, not to obscure the story, but to draw out the implications of it. They dealt with the unraveling implications involved in the story of redemption.

Story, then, is basic in the Bible. Charles Rice pegged it: "The Old Testament reaches its high water marks in the telling and retelling of the story of a people freed and given a new land, and the New Testament, for all its diverse complexity, is the passion narrative writ large."[2]

The narrative base of the biblical literature spawned the narrative nature of first-century preaching. At that time, as Wardlaw* says,

---

*From the Introduction, "The Need for New Shapes," in *Preaching Biblically*, Don M. Wardlaw, ed., (Philadelphia: The Westminster Press, 1983).

the controlling structure of Christian preaching was narrative, the recollection of what God in Christ had done, was doing, would do to intervene graciously in human affairs. Reflection on the implications of that story for its hearers followed, usually in the form of exhortations and combined the synagogue's tradition of interpreting scripture with pleas for behavioral change. The preacher concentrated on re-creating holy history, intermixing the recital with the "now, therefore," of ethical demand. Narration regulated sermon design. Reflection, application, and impassioned exhortation took their places along story line.[3]

The Loss of "Story" in Preaching

Unfortunately, various factors which impacted Christian preaching obscured the story dimension of the Bible. Together, they all but submerged the basically narrative nature of Christian preaching.

Doctrinal Controversies

During the patristic period the church became preoccupied with verbal formulas, connotations, and nuances of words in an effort to hammer out precise statements of theological truth. The result was that propositional truth overlayed the dynamic dimension native to the gospel. What the church accomplished in the first four ecumenical conferences needed to be done. Unfortunately, the side-effect was an emphasis on static words to the neglect of the dynamic Word. The focus shifted from the story to the interpretation of the story. When the church became preoccupied with verbal formulas it ran the risk of losing the dynamic of the gospel story.

Rhetorical Theory

The fusion of Christian preaching with classical rhetorical theory compounded the problem. As the church conquered the Hellenistic world, Greek and Roman rhetorical theory conquered the sermon.

The situation was solidified by Augustine (354-430), who wrote what is commonly agreed to be the first textbook on Christian preaching, book 4 of *On Christian Doctrine*. Early in his life, Augustine had taught rhetoric in Carthage, Rome, and Milan. He drew heavily on the rhetorical principles of Cicero, who in turn had drawn from the ideas of Aristotle. It is understandable, then, that he advised Christian preachers to learn the rules of oratory at an early age by studying the Roman masters or to learn by imitating eloquent men.[4] This wedding between western rhetorical theory and Christian preaching resulted in Scripture texts of various literary forms being forced into a common sermonic mold that had been designed by classical secular rhetorical theory. The loss of the natural diversity in the Bible caused some loss of dynamic in Christian preaching.

The Printing Press

The advent of the printing press profoundly affected the whole society. A "huge significance attached unconsciously and on a culture-wide basis to print as an almost all-out replacement for human-to-human"[5] communication, Henry Mitchell points out. That tended to submerge the story, which is most naturally conveyed by an oral medium.

The Protestant Reformation

While the Reformation helped preaching immensely by its emphasis on a return to the prominence of biblical authority, it provided no help toward a return to the narrative nature of the biblical relevation or the narrative nature of preaching. The chief concerns of the Reformation were theological and ecclesiological, and dogma dominated the sermon.

Each development, then, in the westernization of the sermon led Christian preaching farther away from the basically narrative nature of the gospel. The sermon became fixed rather than fluid, dogmatic rather than dynamic, and logical rather than lively. But a change is on the horizon.

The Recovery of "Story"

Several factors have come together recently pointing to the need for the recovery of the story form of preaching. Some of these factors pertain to human nature. Others relate to present methods of biblical study. No doubt some are cultural in their origin. All point to the fact that the story should be recovered as a valid form for the Christian sermon.

Human Nature

People have always liked a good story. It begins when we're children and want to hear a bedtime story. But kids are not alone. The book, theater, television, and movie industries thrive on people's natural desire for stories. A good story, then, can convey a biblical truth via a medium for which people have an innate affinity.

Biblical Studies

Current biblical studies add force to the movement toward the narrative sermon. The church has always, of course, recognized the narrative nature of much of the biblical literature, even though it has often failed to do justice to the idea hermeneutically and homiletically. More recently, however, biblical studies have acknowledged inherently narrative segments embedded within nonnarrative literary passages. For example, the prominent passage in Philippians 2:5–11 about the *kenosis* of Christ has been identified as a possible New Testament lyric hymn that has been included in the writings of the author in much the same way modern preachers often recite hymns as illustrations in their messages. The passage has an obviously narrative structure.

Recent biblical studies have also emphasized the narrative infrastructure of some nonnarrative biblical literature—the "event" out of which many nonnarrative literary genres came. Additionally, focus is now centering on the

"Christ-event" that serves as the foundation for all of the more formal, literary passages of Scripture. So, an objective view of the nature of the biblical literature highlights the place of narrative in our faith.

The Philosophy of Language

Linguistic studies have reinforced the need for oral, narrative form for the contemporary message. Often, even when traditional preaching has dealt with the variety of biblical literary forms in a responsible way hermeneutically, it has not done so homiletically. It has gone about its business of extracting timeless truths from all sorts of biblical literature and presenting the truths homiletically in a homogeneous way. By the time the sermon is preached, the *form* from which the truth was excavated has been lost. Students of the philosophy of language urge caution against drawing a distinction between a message and the form in which it is presented. A rigid distinction between form and content is "a false distinction. The two cannot really be separated,"[6] according to Amos Wilder. To alter one is in some sense to alter the other. Consequently,

> if the content of Christian proclamation down through the years and today is biblical through and through, the form of Christian proclamation should also be biblical through and through. . . . The biblical character of preaching therefore will determine not only its content but its form . . . , its fabric, . . . its structure. . . . General principles of rhetoric and public address may be helpful in mastering the art of oral communication, but they are subservient to the basic kind of rhetoric used in the Bible because the biblical rhetoric is wedded in form to its content. The fabric or texture of the sermon, as well as its content, will be determined by its biblical roots.[7]

Everyday Life

Life isn't logical. It twists and turns from one event to another. This affirms another call for narrative preaching.

The narrative sermon will be like life. One thing is happening when an authority figure stands up, refers to abstract truths gleaned from a printed page, and objectively states their relevance for life. Another entirely different thing seems to happen when those truths are wrapped up in a human personality or an interesting event. The interest level rises, because most people don't live and function most of the time in realms of ideas or abstractions. They live in the concrete, and they like something colorful. So, sermons should have the feel and sound of personal faith and of event and happening.

The Trend of Our Time

The compatibility of narrative preaching form with our times justifies the story message. We live in a time in which people have been oriented by radio and television to a "story world." The result is that day by day, whether viewers are watching situation comedies, following soap operas, or viewing the news, they are accustomed to following "linear lines" of stories. This "story orientation" of our culture is impacting several areas. "Story" is experiencing a comeback in secular literature. A National Storytelling Festival is conducted annually at Jonesboro, Tennessee, and it has spawned the organization of the National Association for the Preservation and Perpetuation of Storytelling.[8]

As I write this, one of the hottest entertainment items in this video age is—believe it or not—a radio show called "A Prairie Home Companion." There's nothing very fancy about it. Broadcast live from an ordinary place, the World Theatre (which is not as big as it sounds) in an ordinary (by common consent) city, St. Paul, Minnesota—or "on the road" in America's larger cities—it has a down-home assortment of bands, singers, and comedians. The centerpiece of each show is Garrison Keillor's delivery of the news from the imaginary little town of Lake Wobegon. Keillor's "news" is usually a cleverly woven tale about what's happening at the P.T.A. meeting or the local grocery, the parish house or the corner cafe. Nothing much to it, right? Wrong. The show, broadcast on National Public Radio, is carried by as many as 260 U.S. public radio stations plus stations in Australia. When Keillor compiled several of his stories into a book entitled, suitably enough, *Lake Wobegon Days*, it spurted to the *New York Times'* best-seller list.

Narrative isn't confined to the entertainment world. It is sweeping the field. Elie Wiesel is the center of a growing cluster of serious contemporary storytellers. Contemporary theology is experiencing a trend toward "narrative theology," and communication theory is now viewed from the angle of a "shared story."[9] Story is in.

In such a narrative-oriented setting, the typical sermonic monologue about abstract truths can seem rather sterile and static. The contemporary mindset is particularly sensitized to receive a narrative sermon, one that has the feel of life, movement, and drama.

12

Finding the Story Message

IF YOU'VE WORKED A LONG TIME from only the traditional perspective, your first challenge will be to find the biblical basis for a narrative sermon. Perhaps you've looked so long at the biblical literature through homiletical glasses that you have a hard time recognizing the essentially narrative structure of much biblical material.

The Narrative Message from Narrative Biblical Literature

The obvious place to find the biblical basis for a narrative sermon is the Bible's narrative literature. As mentioned earlier, a vast amount of biblical literature is narrative in structure. This is not only true of the historical segments of the Bible, but also of parables, legends, allegories, examples, stories, and similar passages. These all have a basically narrative form.

The Narrative in One Passage

Frequently, a narrative message can be based upon the story found in a single location in Scripture. It may be either a brief passage or a rather lengthy one.

Here the structuring of the message is simple, requiring

no transformation at all. In most cases, you will find that the biblical writer has done a rather good job of telling the story in order to accomplish his purpose. Therefore, you can structure the message just as he structured the Scripture. It may help, however, from time to time to rearrange some of the particulars within the story in order to heighten or intensify the thrust of the message. Several types of story may be found in a single text.

1. The story of a *person (or persons)* related in a single biblical passage is an obvious source. The Bible is a book about life, and human personality walks across the pages of the Bible as large as life. There they are—the variety of people good and bad, old and young, strong and weak— they all catch human interest.

2. The story of a biblical *event* is useful, also. Some biblical stories center around events more than people. People are involved, but they are not the point of the story. The confrontation between Elijah and the priests and prophets of Baal at Mt. Carmel focuses, not on Elijah, but on the crisis of the confrontation between false gods and the true God. You could retell the story primarily from the perspective of Elijah, but it may be more to the point of the passage to focus on the event, allowing Elijah and the priests and prophets of Baal to be the tributaries that flow into the stream of events at the altar on the top of the mountain. What drama, what vivid imagery can be woven into this story! The story of the marriage of Ahab and Jezebel, along with the importation of the gods of Jezebel can be used to set the stage. The geographical location of Mt. Carmel, looking to the southeast upon the fertile plain of Jezreel and to the west upon the blue Mediterranean—what a high point in the history of Israel.

3. Stories of a *succession of events* in a long passage can be woven into a single narrative message. Think of the possibilities of storytelling that lie in the drama of the battles of the Israelite people at Jericho and Ai (Joshua 6 and 7). Al-

though an artificial break between the two stories appears in our Bibles because of the division between chapters 6 and 7 of the book of Joshua, the two were obviously intended by the writer to be taken together. Notice the adversative conjunction that begins chapter 7. On the one hand, elaborate preparation preceded the battle of Jericho. Huge crowds became involved. They used strange tactics. The walls tumbled in.

The very next battle was for the relatively obscure village of Ai. They didn't use many troops. They made no elaborate preparations. And they lost the battle. The point of the story? The difference between victory and defeat lies in the presence or absence of God with his people. Obviously, this story centers more on events than on people—more on Jericho and Ai than on Joshua or Achan.

The Narrative from Several Passages

It isn't necessary to limit the biblical source for a narrative sermon to only one biblical source. Several possibilities suggest themselves for a narrative message based on separate, but related, Scripture passages.

1. The story of a *person (or persons) mentioned in several biblical passages* can yield a narrative message. For example, you could build a challenging sermon around the three places where Demas is mentioned in the Bible. He is first named in Colossians 4:14 and Philemon 24, with Paul acknowledging that he is a companion and a fellow laborer during one of Paul's imprisonments. Then, in 2 Timothy 4:10, which reflects the situation of Paul's later imprisonment, Paul said: "Demas, having loved this present world, has deserted me." Here the plot line of the sequence of Scriptures follows the normal layout of a tragedy of a promising beginning followed by a dismal failure.

On the other hand, you could strike a more positive note by the story of Aquila and Priscilla. Acts 18 records that these two first met Paul at Corinth. A good deal of material is available about their having left Italy because of the Emperor Claudius's order expelling the Jews from Rome. With good research into the subjects of Rome and Claudius, this could be developed into a very interesting part of the story. This same reference tells that they hosted Paul and shared the tentmaking trade with him. They were together eighteen months. Trouble broke out. They left together for Ephesus on the way to Syria.

The next glimpse we get of this couple is of their continued companionship and encouragement of Paul in Ephesus, but we don't find that in Acts. As Paul concluded the first letter to the Corinthian Christians (probably written from Ephesus) he told the Corinthians, "Aquila and Prisca greet you heartily in the Lord, with the church that is in their house" (1 Cor. 16:19). At Ephesus they met Apollos and instructed him more completely in Christian doctrine (Acts 18:26). After that they seem to have returned to Rome, for when Paul wrote the Roman letter he told the Christians there to "greet Prisca and Aquila," people who had "risked their own necks" for the sake of the gospel (Rom. 16:3–4). This couple had shown courage both in Corinth when the uprising among the Jews occurred and in Ephesus when the uprising occurred among the craftsmen because Paul's preaching was having a detrimental effect upon their trade. Finally, they must have left Rome again, for in 2 Timothy 4:19, Paul, now imprisoned in Rome, sends greetings to them through Timothy. What an exciting couple this must have been! Few messages have been preached about them. Yet their story can deeply move and motivate the hearer today.

I point to the examples of Demas, Aquila, and Priscilla because they are relatively unknown, obscure characters. The intention is to show how you can base a narrative message on several passages of Scripture. When you turn to the more prominent figures who are mentioned many times in the Bible, the opportunities for narrative messages that are the stories of people based on more than one text are plentiful.

2. Stories of *places mentioned in several biblical references* provide an interesting alternative. Think about Jericho, which has a story of its own, being one of the oldest continually inhabited cities in the world.

Present to your people, based upon good research, the nature of life in Jericho before the Israelite conquest. Following that, tell the drama of the siege of Jericho by the Israelite armies, focusing on the truth that the power of God was manifest in that city. Then, move to stories of Jericho recorded in the New Testament. It was in this city that Christ healed blind Bartimaeus. The poignancy of the healing of the blind man has powerful drama in it. The story points to the same truth embedded in the Old Testament story—the power of God. But it focuses more clearly upon the fact that God uses his power, not only for the conquest of cities, but also for the compassionate cure of an individual.

Consider also two interesting times Joppa is mentioned in the Bible. Jonah 1:3 relates that Jonah used it as a jumping off place to run from God's call to prophesy to non-Jewish people. Acts 10 tells us that in Joppa Peter learned his lesson that God could consider the gentiles clean. You could weave the stories of those two episodes into a message about missions.

3. *Separate biblical events having a single focus* offer another possibility. Several narratives in different parts of the Bible point to an identical truth. You could reconstruct and tell these together; telling the subsequent events would reinforce the truth highlighted by the first event.

Narrative Segments in Nonnarrative Scripture

Narratively structured segments embedded within nonnarrative literature provide another source for a story sermon. The previously mentioned passage in Philippians

2:6–11 is an obvious instance of a narratively structured segment within epistolary literature. Whether you believe that this was originally a hymn sung by the early church, as suggested by some form critics, it is undeniably narrative-like in structure. The story carries high drama! What excitement can be experienced in sharing what can be considered as the three acts of the drama of Christ: Christ equal with God, Christ experiencing humanity, and Christ exalted in the universe!

Another example of narratively structured literature embedded in nonnarrative literature is Galatians 1:13–24. In his letter to the Galatian Christians, broaching the subject of the Judaizing controversy, Paul narrates to his readers a synopsis of his life from the moment of his conversion to the midpoint of his missionary career. This, of course, covers a larger segment of time than the account of his conversion in the book of Acts. What we know of the conversion part of his story from Acts could be integrated into that part of the story rehearsed in Galatians.

In light of the several approaches suggested above, ample biblical material is available to give you a start in narrative preaching. It may prove rather easy and quite refreshing to begin to free the biblical narratives from the domination of Greek rhetorical forms.

The Narrative Message from Nonnarrative Biblical Literature

Several who are currently working in preaching theory suggest that narrative sermons need not be based solely on narrative biblical literature. The fascination with "story" has prompted research into ways of developing narrative sermons from other types of biblical literature. However, caution is in order at this point. Advocates of narrative preaching have severely criticized traditional homiletics for forcing the narrative biblical literature into molds and forms alien to it. Would not those who press all biblical literature into the "story" homiletical mold be committing the same error as those whom they criticize?

With caution urged, let me make some suggestions. Those who want to go beyond these possibilities will find available suggestions concerning the "translation into narrative form" of other literary genres.[10]

Events Behind a Nonnarrative Text

A story line can be found often in the background of a nonnarrative text. It has been pointed out that literary genre

> such as law codes, prophetic oracles, and wisdom sayings, (sic) presuppose for their understanding certain stories or situations in the ancient communities of the faithful. It is sometimes vivid and useful to sketch the story out of which the saying grew rather than to plunk it down in the pulpit like a chicken without feathers. In its full context we see and feel its power as a part of a real human story, and not simply as a disembodied spiritual or ethical principle.[11]

An example may help. Traditionally, preachers using a biblical exhortation such as "rejoice in the Lord always" (Phil. 4:4) will launch immediately into a sermon derived primarily from their minds, revolving around such logical categories as why we should rejoice, and what we should rejoice about. The vitality of the message of the particular Scripture may be lost this way. "This exhortation takes on its fundamental meaning only when we see Paul dictating those lines from prison, facing imminent death."[12] You could reconstruct the series of imprisonments Paul had experienced before this one. Then describe realistically, but dramatically, the particular dimensions of this imprisonment from which the Philippian letter came. Paul's encouragement to rejoice bears real credentials when we realize it is coming, not from ivory tower philosophy, but from a man who has been in prison again and again. Tell those stories. *Then* share the text.

A reconstruction of the historical story out of which an exclamation, exhortation, or injunction in Scripture is recorded will often provide a wide-open door to "story lines" behind texts. As long as integrity is maintained with the story actually behind the text and to the meaning of the text itself, no violation of sound exegesis and hermeneutic occurs.

Imagined Situations

A story line based on imagined situations implied in the text can be used. Philippians 4:4 will serve again as the example.

Begin, not with *this* text, but with Acts 16. Retell the story of the conversion to faith of the jailer in Philippi, carefully pointing out that "about midnight Paul and Silas were . . . singing hymns of praise to God" (Acts 16:25). Emphasize the fact that it says that "he [the jailer] was baptized, he and all his household" (Acts 16:33).

Imaginatively reconstruct a typical family belonging to the jailer. Here they are, Christians in Philippi. It must have been difficult. Clearly there was antagonism to the believers in Jesus. An ugly situation had developed. Paul and Silas had been dragged into the marketplace before the authorities. Philippi was a Roman colony; there weren't many Jews there to begin with. Being a *gentile* who had responded to the message of a *Jewish* man must have been an awkward thing. Reconstruct what it was like to be a Philippian jailer who was a Christian. Imagine what it was like for his wife and his son and his daughter—and perhaps for his servants. It would be clear that being a Christian was not easy for these people.

Having reconstructed the difficulties of being a Christian in Philippi, now make your move to Philippians 4:4. Picture the Philippian Christians, among them the jailer and his family, receiving a letter from Paul. In it they read: "Rejoice in the Lord always; again I will say, rejoice!"

(Phil. 4:4). Then you could imaginatively retell how each family member went back into that difficult situation which you earlier described. Tell how their renewed joy enabled them to cope with their difficult situations.

Why was that possible? Why was the admonition credible? Because they knew that the one who had rejoiced even while in jail in their city was now in jail either in Rome or Caesarea (depending on your view), writing to them. His admonition to rejoice had credibility because he was speaking out of the crucible of difficulty himself.

This weaving together of historical fact, incidents in relation to one another, and appropriately controlled imagination of mood and feeling conspire to bring together a story sermon consistent with and not contrary to exegetical facts.

Story of a "Motif"

A story line can be found occasionally by tracing an idea in a text through the different times the idea or concept occurs in Scripture. For example, a message with a narrative structure could be based on the statement: "Now is the Son of Man glorified" (John 13:31).[13] The message could revolve around biblical narratives of other events in the life of Christ when other people thought it was time for his glory. The disciples were always thinking: "Now is the time for his glory!"

One such episode revolved around the incident of the feeding of the crowd with a little bread and a few fish. According to the narrative (John 6:1–15) the crowd perceived this as a sign and "they were intending to come and take Him by force, to make Him king" (John 6:15). They thought this was the time and the event for his glory. But he "withdrew again to the mountain by Himself alone." It was not yet time for his glory.

Later, the event of his transfiguration occurred. Reconstruct the event of Peter, James, John, and Jesus atop the mountain. This was a great moment in Jesus' life. Peter said:

"Master, it is good for us to be here; and let us make three tabernacles: one for You, and one for Moses, and one for Elijah" (Luke 9:33). It obviously was a moment of glory. The *Shekinah* was there. But the writer of Luke editorializes upon Peter's comment by adding that Peter spoke "not realizing what he was saying" (Luke 9:33b). Peter thought it was time for Christ's glory. But it was not yet time.

Then, the message could move from that mountaintop to a city in the mountains, Jerusalem, where the words of the text were spoken. The setting for the text is the Last Supper. Jesus is now in the shadow of the cross. When the betrayer had left the scene, Jesus said: "Now is the Son of Man glorified. . . ." What a strange kind of glory—the glory of death! But after death, resurrection!

In this approach, put the biblical text appropriately in its place among surrounding incidents in Scripture related to the same idea. Then put the text in its own historical setting for emphasis and clarity.

Similes and Metaphors

A story line for a narrative sermon can be found in the use of a scriptural simile or metaphor as a "window on eventfulness" through which you look back on the "parade of holy history" and see events in the Bible where the metaphor or its meaning recurs.[14]

John 21:15–19 can serve as an example. In it, Jesus tells Simon Peter to feed the sheep.

What did Jesus mean by this key metaphor "feed"? Feeding obviously is an experience of nurturance we first learn in our mother's arms, the other side of the coin of trust. When we look through the "trust/feed" window on the parade of God's story, we see manna from heaven for wandering Israelites; we see a picture of a banquet on a mountain (Isaiah 25) as God's future deliverance; the feeding of the 5000; the feeding of the disciples in the Upper Room; we even see Jesus feeding the disciples breakfast on the beach before he asked Peter to feed His sheep. What we have is a parade of feedings eliciting trust in God. An imaginative sermon on that metaphor could recreate several of these feedings in narrative form to enable us to experience the feeding God calls us to offer.[15]

The Narrative Message
Incorporating Biblical Themes

Some are advocating and preaching story sermons that are biblical in the sense that they convey concepts and ideas consistent with the biblical revelation, but not based on any particular passage of Scripture. These might best be called sermonic creative fiction. The creativity needed, combined with the demands of time and discipline involved, make this type of work virtually inaccessible to most preachers. A few, however, can do it very well. Help is available for those who want to try.[16]

13

Researching the Story

HAVING FOUND THE STORY LINE, you will need to discover the focus of the story and identify its human interest features.

The Point of the Story

An attempt at a story message can result in a meaningless recounting of trivia if it has no integrating factor and clear focus. There's no point in telling the story unless the people get the point, and they won't get the point unless *you* get the point.

A good deal of discipline in critical exegesis may be required in order to identify the point of the story. This is particularly true with a message based upon a biblical narrative. Those of us who grew up in church have heard these stories again and again. The Sunday School teacher, parent, or preacher bequeathed to us a clear impression of the moral of the story. The points they identified may or may not be the accurate ones; careful exegesis will have to determine that. Some guidelines may be helpful.

The Intentional Factor

We have already noticed that there were more stories in Israel than the Old Testament record included and that the

New Testament writers did not write about everything Jesus did (John 21:25). The biblical writers did as all historians and biographers have done. They used some principles of selectivity in the decision about what to record and what to leave out. Your challenge is to find what the biblical writer intended to convey by including it.

A significant clue to the answer may lie in the overall purpose of the biblical book in which the story occurs. Biblical scholarship has for a long time recognized the general direction or purpose of various biblical books. Such information is found in introductory volumes to the Old and New Testaments and in the general background sections usually preceding the exegetical sections of commentaries. Clues to the intended meaning of a particular passage may lie in the relationship it has to the entire book.

Additional help in identifying the point of the story may be found by consulting the works representative of a recent trend in biblical studies, redaction criticism, which focuses on the theological intent involved in the biblical writer's selection of which narratives to include and the editorial processes used in narrating the event.

Among the processes used in this endeavor, one method is to examine the "external boundaries" of your text. The constituent components of the Gospels, for example, are not just random stories loosely strung together; rather, a continuity runs through them, and the intended theology of your text may be illuminated by the adjacent passages and the way they are joined by introductory words or concluding summaries. For example, it may be of more than passing interest that the parable of the good Samaritan in Luke 10 follows the account in Luke 9 of Jesus' rebuke of James and John for their anger at the inhospitable Samaritan village. This is even more interesting in light of the gentile Luke's purpose to show Jesus as a universal Savior, in contrast to Matthew's purpose to show him as the Messiah.[17]

Beyond the examination of the external boundaries, the

"internal distinctives" of your passage may serve as a clue to the theological intent of the writer. This would be particularly true when the account of an incident in one of the synoptic Gospels differs from another. Obviously each author adapted the common material (whether shared or independently acquired) in order to focus on a particular interest and perspective.

Another recent trend in biblical studies, structuralism, is helpful at this point. Its working procedure is to analyze a unit of Scripture with a view to discovering significant clues in the structure of the passage or in signals within it that point to the central thought of the passage. Certain phenomena can be significant clues to the centrality and pervasiveness of a thought in the entire passage—phenomena such as the repetition of words, repetition of concepts with synonymous words, coordinate conjunctions, a subordinate clause at the beginning of a sentence containing material related to the preceding sentence, a correlative adverb that "reaches back" into a preceding sentence, or a pronoun having an antecedent in a preceding sentence.[18]

The same kind of examination can be useful for biblical literature other than the synoptics. For example, Acts 27:39 through 28:6 narrates the dramatic story of the shipwreck and survival of Paul and his company on the island of Malta. Here there is a highly sensory and dramatic description of natives, fires, snakes, and frightened soldiers. So far, it's just an interesting story. But what of it? What's the point of the story? Perhaps the point is found when you go behind chapter 28 to chapter 27, which has the account of the beginnings of the trouble in the story of the storm off the shore of Crete, before the shipwreck at Malta. While the men were frightened, Paul spoke to them and told them that "an angel of God" appeared before him in the night saying: "Do not be afraid, Paul; you must stand before Caesar; and behold, God has granted you all those who are sailing with you" (Acts 27:24).

Could it be, then, that the purpose of the writer of the book of Acts in telling the story of the shipwreck and survival lay in the truth of the providence of God—that God could work through the difficulties of the storm to preserve the safety of Paul in order that he might reach Rome? Translated, the truth is that God is able and careful to preserve those who trust him and see them through to his purpose for them. Nothing ultimately frustrates the will of God.

The Eternal Factor

Ask what eternal truth or truths are embedded in this narrative. Remember that a narrative is a story of what did happen one time. It is descriptive, not prescriptive. Don't make the narrative normative. Don't elevate the incidental to the eternal.

The Quantitative Factor

Throughout the history of biblical interpretation, there has been a tendency to allegorize the narratively structured literature by finding far more meanings tucked into the corners than were put there by the author. Remember the distinction between narrative and allegory. You may want to ask yourself: "How many points am I getting out of this story? Did the writer really put them there? If he heard my message, would he be surprised by my interpretation of the meaning of what he said?"

Enhancing the Story

For interest sake, you will need to do more than recite the bare facts of the story. You will need to fill the role of the "color commentator." Such a person does extensive research into the lives of the athletes seen in play on the TV screen; likewise you will need to research thoroughly the characters and incidents of the story.

Think in terms of *enhancing* the story by an imagination stimulated and controlled by research rather than *embellishing* the story by unrestrained imagination. While imagination is an indispensable tool in story building, it does not have to take the form of unbridled fantasizing. Disciplined research into the biblical material can provide enough stimulus for the imagination to work in concert with the realities of the text. Strive for responsible imagination.

Careful research along the same lines suggested for the dramatic monologue should be done in preparation for the narrative message. Several suggestions designed to help you get into the biblical narratives follow.[19]

Read Every Line

Most of us already carry in our minds the pivotal segments and large "chunks" that comprise the structure of familiar biblical stories. We are tempted to take our first impressions and simply go with these, reciting the already familiar dimensions of the story. In doing so, we may miss something significant, a new point of view.

1. You may notice in an apparently ordinary line something very significant. For example, a not-so-prominent line in the parable of the prodigal son offers great possibilities for conveying the mood and point of the story, the father's love. As the story unfolds, the older son, upon seeing the party inside and being told it was in honor of the young prodigal, "became angry, and was not willing to go in" (Luke 15:28). Then, the same father who "ran and embraced" the prodigal son (v. 20) "came out and began entreating" (v. 28) the elder son. But how many sermons have you heard emphasizing that the father *came out to both* sons? The father loved the stay-at-home as much as he loved the prodigal.

2. You may notice an apparently insignificant character or event. In many of the biblical narratives, several

characters are involved; in the larger event are several incidents. But our memory of the story has focused on a simple, obvious movement, often to the neglect of the "minor" events or persons in the story. A great deal of meaning can be derived from giving due place to some of the specifics we have frequently overlooked.

Read Behind the Lines

Research the external situations behind the text, and get into the dynamics beneath the surface.

1. Read the story in light of its milieu. Research of the socioeconomic, political, and religious structures behind an incident can help you and your hearers understand *why* some things in the story happened as they did. Why did it seem so incredible to the Samaritan woman that Jesus would talk with her (John 4)? Only if you provide your hearers insight into the sociology behind her question will they understand the poignancy of the situation.

2. Read the story in light of your own experience.

Often we find it difficult to identify with a story's "villain"— who obviously is wrong, immoral, etc. So the Prodigal Son generally is portrayed as a rebellious teenager who flippantly tells his father that he wants to "do his own thing." Likewise the elder son is painted as a stubborn petulant one who never sins and never forgives. But have you ever left home for a *good* reason; or have you grown weary of special treatment to the undeserving? If so, you can enter the story with empathy for both sons, and your hearers will join you there. If a narrative contains events and material outside your experience, imagine someone you know and respect who has had such experiences.[20]

3. Read the story looking for motives behind behavior.

The prodigal stays or leaves but the cumulative reasons for each may reveal only a slight edge of one over the other. The behavior of the Pharisee in the Pharisees and Publican narrative appears on the surface so vain and self-serving as to make him uncredible—a conclusion which is reason enough to ask if there are not other motives at work. In the process of our looking for the internal motives he will begin to look more and more like the rest of us. The issue is not to find excuses for unethical or otherwise inappropriate behavior, but to ascertain the causative factors in order to a) help the listeners identify with the character, and b) establish a credible context in which the Gospel can be relevantly heard.[21]

4. Read the story looking for the dynamic behind it.

Facts, like still shots of moving objects, may prove helpful for close scrutiny but almost invariably distort the experiential reality. Whatever conclusion one may draw about the betrayal by Judas, it must be set within the context of his being a trusted and ongoing member of the group of disciples. Likewise, Jesus perceived more than immediately available facts when he came across the man at the pool of Bethsaida *(sic)* and asked: "Do you want to be healed?" (John 5:6)[22]

Similarly, it would be easy to inject into the parable of the prodigal son the normal dynamics of sibling rivalry known by your own experiences or by your study of psychology.

Read Between the Lines

Stop between the explicit actions long enough to imagine the implicit action. For instance, Zaccheus was invited down out of the tree. We are told a bit about the crowd's reaction, and then are whisked quickly away to Zaccheus' house. But wait a minute. What did Zaccheus think and feel after Jesus addressed him and before he received him joyfully? How did he get out of the tree? And what did he and Jesus talk about as they walked to his home? The narrative doesn't say—and we are given a chance for our imagination to paint the picture.[23]

Read Yourself into the Story

Try to empathize with the various characters as you read the story several times. You may find it helpful to drop all inhibitions and in some private place, role play each character in the text. This can provide some perspective or initiate a feeling or open an angle that you would not get by simply reading the material.

As you empathize with the people involved in the story, the story will become more lifelike. The more you get into the story, the more your hearers will get out of the story.

14

Developing the Story Message

HAVING RESEARCHED THE MATERIAL relevant to the story and discovered its human dimensions, you are now ready to build the message. That requires two things—deciding on a plot and writing the story.

Plotting the Story

What shape should the message have? How should it be structured? Various forms can be utilized, depending on whether you opt for indirect or direct application.

Indirect Application

Indirect application can be designed in two ways.

1. The first is a "single-layer" approach. In it you simply retell the biblical story in its enhanced form, leaving it to the hearers to identify its relevance to them.

2. The second is a "two-layer" approach in which you parallel the biblical story with a contemporary version of essentially the same story (either a true one or a piece of created fiction). It could still be left to the hearers to spot the relevance and see themselves in the contemporary version. In either approach the sequence of the components of the story can vary.

If you elect to use the two-layer approach, three basic overarching frameworks are possible.

One approach would be to tell the story twice, telling it in its original setting the first time and then retelling it in twentieth-century dress. You need to be sure to inject good human interest elements of the story into the first telling, so that the biblical story won't seem relatively uninteresting as compared to the modern story. If that happens, you run the risk of losing your people before you get to the relevance of the message.

A second basic approach simply

> reverses the above, beginning with a contemporary narrative or problem situation that is an unannounced cultural translation of the pericope. Reflective moments in the action raise issues that prepare us now to hear the original scriptural text for clues for resolving the story or situation with which we began.

A more challenging and imaginative approach lies in intermingling

> biblical with contemporary times, moving through the narrative by intercutting scene by scene between the first and twentieth centuries. We thus accentuate through such a fantasy the fact that the first and twentieth centuries, while of a different *chronos* [era of time], nevertheless share the same *kairos* [kind of time].[24]

With any of these approaches, you have two additional options.

1. A story message following the sequence of the biblical narrative is the obvious possibility. An abundance of biblical material with essentially narrative structure can be presented effectively in the same way the Scripture narrates the elements. In these cases the text provides the structure of the message. The components of the story follow the line of the text.

2. A narrative message rearranging the sequence of components in the biblical narrative is also possible. Start with the climactic episode of a narrative. Ask, How did this happen? Then move back to the beginning and trace the development of the biblical narrative, arriving again at the climactic episode, which would receive briefer treatment this time.

Direct Application

A structure designed for more direct application could take either of two forms. The first is a partial narrative sermon in which the large part of the sermon, the enhanced biblical narrative, would be followed by a relatively brief application and conclusion of the meaning of the story. The second possibility is an alternating narrative sermon in which you stop along the way in the story to apply various segments of the story to the lives of your hearers.

Writing the Story

With the structure in mind, flesh out the message by providing content to accomplish the two-dimensional nature of preaching in a style compatible with storytelling.

The Content of the Message

1. With reference to the biblically related message content, the same types of material useful in the dramatic monologue message are useful in the narrative sermon. The material is simply conveyed in the third person rather than from the first person perspective. Retell the story, stopping to dwell at certain points along the way where the dimensions of the story convey the thrusts of your message. Be sure to provide humanizing features of sensory descriptions, empathetic feelings, and characterizations of the people in the story.

2. With reference to life-related message content, the question arises again concerning the relative merits of direct

and indirect application. You will have to decide whether
the story can convey its own meaning or if you need to interpret its meaning for your congregation.

a) Craddock argues for application by indirection or
implication. He says that narrative sermons "do not sum-
marize events . . . with commentary and application following."[25] Support for the argument is sometimes based on
the psychology of the hearer. Some people, it is felt, have
developed an immunity after being hit so hard repeatedly
with explicit sermon application. The only way they can be
touched is for them to "overhear"—to catch the nuances,
feelings, and subtleties of the story and see themselves in
the picture the preacher draws.

Similarly, some argue for the use of the indicative mood
rather than the hortatory mood in the message. Although
preachers should preach for a verdict, they shouldn't use
"high-pressure hard sell with a person who is callous from
listening day in and day out to high-pressure hard sell.
Moreover, many churchgoers have been led to expect a
dreary procession of musts, oughts, and shoulds which
bounce off their hides like hailstones on concrete."[26] How
then can preachers preach for a verdict? They should
"report the facts of life . . . as accurately, factually, and
imaginatively as possible, then let the Holy Spirit and the
listener work it out from there."[27]

Support for the argument for indirect application is
sometimes based on the biblical models, particularly the
parable. Jesus, it is said, "would begin, 'The kingdom of
heaven is like . . .' and then would follow a crisp, tightly
structured, secular narrative with the issue of it all left in
the lap or in the ears of the listener: 'He that hath ears to
hear, let him hear.'"[28]

Mitchell argues that the authors of the biblical material, chronicling the events in the Old Testament and
New Testament,

put various versions alongside each other in the canon without comment. They must have assumed that folk would get the needed messages on their own. . . . Jesus' own ministry was full of stories, almost none of which required interpretation afterwards. He apparently had the idea that the quaint, simple method of his culture was capable of conveying the greatest profundities, and the impact of his story-telling ministry speaks for itself.[29]

If the preacher is not to explain or apply the story then, who is? Richard Jensen suggests that the open-endedness of a sermon is an open door for the Holy Spirit. He says:

Could we not think of an open-endedness as an openness precisely to the work of the Spirit? Where everything is not spelled out in exact detail perhaps the Spirit of God can move and work with our stories in order that those who hear may hear what it is that God wishes addressed to them.[30]

Words of qualification emerge, however, from some of the advocates of indirect application. Mitchell acknowledges that "as Jesus suggested, *some* interpretation is needed, and this may border on the theological."[31] Also, Jensen acknowledges:

I adhere to this point that the story is the preaching itself in varying degrees. Some stories require additional (from little to much) explanation. Our congregations are simply not prepared to be plunged immediately into story sermons as ends in themselves! Explanation and story need not be juxtaposed to each other as total opposites. Still I would hold out for the possibility that with proper enabling on the part of the preacher all explanations could be dropped. The story can be the preaching itself![32]

Jensen acknowledges that this technique "*is* risky! . . . We cannot know how the people sitting in our pews will complete our story and apply it to their own life [sic]."[33] He verified the risk involved by supervising a project in story-preaching by a graduate student who prepared and presented three story sermons. In the first two, the point of the story was made clear. In the last, it was not. The listeners' responses, he noticed

> were anything but uniform! Each person had completed the sermon for him/herself in a way that fit their own life situation. . . . Rather than getting "his" point, they completed the sermon in such a way that something meaningful happened in their own experience of hearing and reflecting.[34]

The results of this experiment in indirection in homiletics are strikingly similar to the results of the experiments with indirect communication in secular communication theory discussed in the first chapter of this book (see pp. 30–34).

No one would deny that the hearers should "finish out the sermon" by identifying and incorporating into their lives its relevance. But shouldn't what the hearers appropriate to themselves be the relevance of the actual point of the biblical story in its canonical setting? What, other than that, will forestall a rootless subjectivism in which listeners will discover for themselves whatever truth they see in the story and claim biblical authority for their own views?

We're talking about variety in *biblical* preaching which, according to our definition, has a hermeneutical approach strongly integrated with accurate exegesis. The first question in hermeneutics is not, What does that Scripture say to you? The first question is, What *did* that Scripture mean in its canonical setting? The *next* question is, What does *that* (the canonical meaning of the Scripture) mean to the modern hearer?

b) In light of that, others feel a need to provide more direct application. It may be dangerous to leave it to the hearers to negotiate the dilemma of the middle on their own. Some will never make it; they will stay awash out there somewhere. Others may put into shore in the wrong harbor, making a mistaken, destructive interpretation of what *God* meant by what *you* or *I* said (or *didn't* say).

One speaker at the 1979 meeting of the Academy of Homiletics, which was devoted to the subject of "Preaching and Story," noted that there is a "serious risk in our fascination with story," and suggested that "we may try to make story do more than story can really do." His argument for more "substantive interpretation" of the story also appealed to the biblical models of parabolic literature.

> Some studies of the parables point to this. It is easy to make too great a claim for this form of narration. The whole Christian Gospel is not communicated in the parables of Jesus. Moreover, the records indicate that the parables were not always understood. Even his parables required explanation, and indeed they required the sermons and epistles of his followers.

The speaker reached the conclusion that "the Gospel is event and meaning; . . . authentic preaching is story and interpretation."[35]

Other facts about the parables are worth noticing. Those who first heard the parables heard them told *in their setting*. They were aware of the situation that spawned the story. So, for many of them, the setting clearly articulated the focus of the meaning of the parable.

In other cases, their immediate involvement in the cultural milieu of the parable enabled them to understand. But in our technocratic society, we may be totally oblivious to innuendoes and nuances that would have been obvious to them in an agrarian society.

Also, of course, some of the parables are interpreted in Scripture itself. Regardless of whether the parables were interpreted when originally spoken, *as we have them* they frequently are accompanied by an editorial comment about their meaning. Somewhere along the line prior to their inclusion in the canon, the believing community believed they needed interpretation. Occasionally the Gospel writers supplied the interpretation, often attributed to Jesus. The parable of the rich man, for example, concluded with the statement: "So is the man who lays up treasure for himself, and is not rich toward God" (Luke 12:21). Similar editorial comments of interpretation follow several of the parables.

Recently, Richard Lischer pointed out "the limits of story" and asked an incisive question:

> How many of our sermons end either with an "intelligent understanding" or an aesthetic "wonder at" without echoing the ringing call to change so characteristic of New Testament and classical preaching? Only in the Gnostic Gospels does Jesus counsel salvation by introspection.[36]

Perhaps all of this is enough to offer a word of caution about assuming that the story can occupy all of the sermon. If the message is to be accurately perceived, you may need to articulate clearly the principle(s) or truth(s) conveyed by the story. This can be done without getting into detailed, lengthy application of the truth to the various areas of the lives of the hearers. Just focus on the main truth. It is at this point that the sermon can be left with the people and the Spirit of God.

The Style of the Message

Unfortunately, the language of a typical sermon is usually not at all like the language of a story. Preachers tend to write sermons with literary style rather than messages with oral style. Writing the story message will require, for many, getting out of the groove into which we have dug ourselves with pencils and typewriters. At this point we can learn from the biblical narratives as well as from the basic style of the secular narrative.

1. The style of the biblical narratives is a good model. Notice several things about them.

a) Biblical narratives normally use normal language. We have "holyized" Scripture to the point that we are not able to recognize or reproduce the human dimensions of it. Notice the language of the narratives in Scripture. The Old Testament very frankly tells stories revolving around "battles and sex, and death, and shady deals, . . . markets and temples and idols and courts and deserts and cities. And this is where the 'spiritual' is discerned, not apart from it."[37] The New Testament confronts us with the fact that Jesus told ordinary, secular, worldly stories about farmers finding treasure, young men running away from home, and plants growing. If our sermons are to sound biblical then, the

> fabric of the sermon will be worldly, secular, through and through. "The language of Canaan," [our holy talk] the . . . smoke screen which hides and distorts the Gospel . . . , will be replaced by the actual language of the Bible, the *true* "language of Canaan," the language and idioms of the people where they are, the vernacular, the vocabulary of the world in which we live."[38]

b) Biblical narratives use simple, uncluttered language. In the biblical stories there is "no wordiness," but the language is "lean and spare, the narrative making its point briefly and sharply."[39] This will call for the omission of a good deal of the language normally used in preaching. It brushes away, among other things, labored rhetorical devices such as alliteration, assonance, and flourishing adjectives. The nouns and the verbs carry the story.

c) Biblical narratives often include dialogue. Lowry points out that Jesus could have told the story of the prodigal son's return in a very prosaic way by saying "the son decided to return home, confess his sin, and ask for a job." Instead, Jesus alternated between the third- and the first-person singular language. Notice the switch:

> But when he came to himself he said, "How many of my
> father's hired servants have bread enough and to spare, but
> I perish here with hunger! I will arise and go to my father,
> and I will say to him, 'Father, I have sinned against heaven
> and before you; I am no longer worthy to be called your
> son; treat me as one of your hired servants.'" And he arose
> and came to his father (Luke 15:17–20a).

This is not an unusual stylistic device. Many times the
writers of the biblical narratives switched persons.

   d) Biblical narratives use sensory language.

> Jesus portrayed vividly the scene of the prodigal's home-
> coming party so that the elder son and the rest of us could
> hear the music, see the dancing and smell the food. Utiliza-
> tion of the sense in storytelling is not a cheap device for
> "effect"; it is the entree to participation for the listener.[40]

At this point the empathy mentioned before comes into
play. The way to utilize senses is by empathizing with the
personality involved in the story. Imagine what he would
see, feel, hear, smell, or touch in his situation.

   2. In addition to learning our sermonic style from biblical narratives, a study of secular narrative style is helpful.
Read contemporary fiction. From it you will learn several
things.

   a) Achieve a proper mix between the specifics of the
story, which will provide "concretion" for the hearers, and
generalities, which will provide perspective for them. Arrange the components of the story in such a way that there
are undulations between concrete specifics and larger generalities. Omitting the details will run the risk of loss of
human interest. Omitting the larger issues will run the risk
of missing the point of the story.

   b) Write in such a way as to bounce appropriately
back and forth between the "inner world" of the story—
the moods and feelings of the characters—and the "outer
world" of the story—the dimensions of the event.

c) It will help sometimes to set the stage early in the story for a major dimension that will come later. After you have gained a perspective on the flow of the story and its components, identify the high points of the story. Then go back and touch up the writing so that you foreshadow the important thing that is to come. In this approach, "in order to highlight the importance of a later event, the storyteller gives an earlier but then unrecognizable clue. When the later moment is reached in the process of the telling, it becomes highlighted by the prior remark."[41] For example, one of the highlights of the story of the prodigal son comes at this point in the story: "But when he came to his senses, he said . . . 'I will get up and go to my father'" (Luke 15:17–18). On that peg the story turns. You can foreshadow that event earlier in the story by "playing on" his encounter with his father *before* leaving as follows:

> So he's done it now. He's made the decision. He went to his father and said: "Father, give me the share of the estate that's mine. I want it now." With family ties as strong as they were in Jewish culture, that was the final act of rebellion. He had no more claim on his family or his father.

By emphasizing ahead of time the complete rupture, you prepare the way for the hearer to feel the magnitude of the love of the father who received him back.

d) Use the active voice and indicative mood rather than the passive voice and subjunctive mood. With tongue in cheek, Lowry points out that Jesus didn't say: "It would be a genuine act of environmental beneficence if the wind velocity were to be reduced through responsiveness to my desire." He said: "Hush, be still!" (Mark 4:39).

e) Use strong verbs, concrete rather than abstract nouns, and verbal contractions when they would normally occur in conversation. Sentence structure is beside the point. To the extent, then, that we've allowed our preaching to become characterized by literary style (which shouldn't be true of any kind of preaching) we'll (not *we shall*) have to change our patterns. We'll have to take to the pulpit the language of the people. We have good precedent for that! Consider Jesus: "The great crowd enjoyed listening to Him" (Mark 12:37). Craddock comments on Jesus' preaching style:

> Here is the Son of God using anecdotes, stories, paradoxes, contradictions, humor, irony, question and answer. Is that the stuff of revelation from on high? It is not the performance that gains tenure or renews contracts. Jesus laid himself open to criticism from even the sophomore class in a rabbinic school, criticism as to scholarship, logic, and systematic consistency. Why did he do it? He gave himself in this sense also, that his communications were servants to awaken, to arouse, to provoke, to assure. Bring to them other canons by which speeches or lectures or sermons are ordinarily measured, and his are hardly classic orations.[42]

15

Telling the Story

THE STEREOTYPICAL IMAGE OF PREACHERS is of pale-faced creatures delivering sermons in sterile environments insulated from the real world by stained-glass windows. The whole scene reeks with the idea that preaching is declamation or oratory.

You're a Storyteller Now

Think of yourself as a storyteller. Because so much of the way we do things comes from a mindset, it will be necessary, perhaps, to set your thinking straight about what is happening while you are preaching the story message. Think of yourself not as an orator, a rhetorician, or a pulpiteer, but as a storyteller. You may need to displace *mentally* your actual physical environment in which you preach, with the typical formal seating arrangement of the listeners sitting side by side in parallel columns while you are on an elevated platform handing something down to them. Instead,

> See [yourself as] the storyteller in the middle of a circle of people; by the lake or around a fire; at the supper table on the evening of the funeral, over food gone cold and dishes

unwashed; one to one, as the story comes out for the first time, the healing time; over breakfast, with the newspaper open, remembering a little girl or boy; on the 4th of July at a picnic, or at home on a snowy day with your grandparents; in a foxhole or a bar, or at the family reunion or around the communion table.[43]

Make It Happen Again

Don't simply *retell* an old story. Attempt to *recreate* it for your hearers. A real storyteller is not merely reporting something that happened or reciting what took place; the speaker is recreating the event with a view to enabling the hearers to relive the experience. But, if they are going to relive it, the storyteller will have to be "reliving the story in imagination even while telling it."[44] You will have to close the gap between the twentieth century and the first century.

Whereas earlier, in the discussion about researching and writing the message, the suggestion was made that you should think of yourself as the color commentator at a football game, at this point—the delivery of the message—you will need to think of yourself as the play-by-play announcer. Now you will have to tell the story as if you are watching it happen, thereby enabling your hearers to watch it happen in their imagination.

Several specific suggestions for storytelling may be helpful. Because the presentation of a message in this way may require significant readjustment of self-image, it may be helpful to do some things designed to get into the mindset productive for story preaching.

1. Use the sensory qualities of language natural to a story. Some of you remember when there was no television. All we had was radio. As we listened to a mystery radio show, the sound-effects men produced at the right time a creaking door, feet walking on a bare plank floor, or the wind whistling through the trees. To augment the sound effects, the script writers wrote dialogue designed

to trigger the hearers' imagination. The result was that we *saw* the story as we listened.

If you have always had television, or have thoroughly immersed yourself in it, it might be helpful to familiarize yourself for the first time with the storytelling kind of language. Fortunately, tapes of some of the old radio shows can now be obtained. Listening to them and getting the feel of language designed to conjure up sensory perception will be helpful in forming methods of oral communication designed to facilitate storytelling.

This will require a change in language style for some, but the change in the language is consistent with the change in the self-image mentioned above.

2. Know the story thoroughly. Storytellers don't need manuscripts. They know the story, they are interested in it, and they are caught up in it to the point that they would never stop to read any part. Such freedom can only come from familiarity with the story. It is seldom important to repeat precisely the sentence structure and the word choices of every detail of our story. It is simply important that we know the story and communicate it.

3. It may be helpful to "do dialogue" in the message. When telling a story, you don't normally say "he said to them" and "they said to her." When you come to the point in the story where you are narrating dialogue that actually happened between persons in the story, speak in the first person as if you were both of the characters involved.

4. It may help to mentally project on an invisible screen in front of you or on the wall behind the congregation a visual image of the action. See the situation; feel the appropriate emotions of all involved; and say their lines, letting your voice naturally follow the shadings of feelings of each person involved in the action. This will add life and vitality to the story. By this means the appropriate human emotions present in the event—anger, embarrassment, courage—can be communicated through the vocal

patterns and inflections. This is a device that will greatly help your hearers to enter into the story as if they are overhearing what is happening.

5. Tell the story naturally. The general sound of the story message will probably be different from the normal sound of a sermon. Unfortunately, some preachers start the story, then automatically gravitate to the old ministerial whine, quiver, or shout. It might help to make it a point to look at the children in the congregation. This will help you drop acquired adult, formal speech patterns that are counterproductive to storytelling.

Specific suggestions about vocalizing the message may be helpful. With the image in mind of yourself as a storyteller in a circle, keep your speech "flexible enough to bend spontaneously to the attentive circle so that the story can become shared story." [45] "A good storyteller is bending to the circle, modifying the details of the narrative, perhaps adding to it, and modulating the voice for these particular listeners." [46]

6. One other suggestion: pace the story properly. In the story there is movement. Sometimes the movement alternates, making fast progress in a short while and then experiencing a lull. The vocal variables of rate, pitch, and volume need to be used so that the sound coming to the hearer is consistent with the content of what is being communicated at the time. Also, the vocal pattern can suggest to the hearer that you have arrived at that part of the story that relates to his or her life. When the story is told effectively, Craddock suggests, "the vocabulary, idiom, imagery, and descriptive detail will be such as will allow points or moments in the process at which the listener can 'enter,' identify, be enrolled. Otherwise . . . [the effort at communication] becomes nothing more than shared information or speech on a certain topic."[47]

In the last analysis, no techniques can guarantee the effectiveness of the narrative message. Pray that God will enable your story to convey The Story.

Part Five

TRY SOMETHING ELSE

Once variety in sermon form and presentation has been introduced effectively to your congregation, you may want to continue exploring additional variations of preaching method. As a matter of fact, some of the sermon forms discussed earlier may seem rather bold changes, and you may feel more comfortable beginning with some of the methods in this section. The approaches discussed here run the gamut from variations in the form of the message to the utilization of technological innovations in its presentation.

16

The Media-Augmented Message

IN ITS EARLY HISTORY, human communication was primarily
by oral means. Sounds were signals, and people told stories
to one another. With the development of the phonetic al-
phabet, communication changed its orientation. It became
sight-oriented. The development of the printing press reinforced that by making available to the masses the printed
page. Ideas supplied the fodder to fill up the pages during
the days of the Enlightenment and following. Communication was "single-channeled": It was conceived of as the
transferal of an idea or concept from one mind to another
by means of the printed page. A single sense, sight, was the
vehicle of communication. Man learned from what he
saw—a static symbol, a printed letter on a page, or a printed picture. A single human faculty, the mind, served as the
receptor of communication.

During this century all of that has changed. First, the
static picture became the silent moving picture. Soon,
sound was added to sight. At first a pianist would accom-
pany the silent picture. Before long, the film had its own
soundtrack. Television brought this phenomenon into our

homes. Recent developments have brought us stereophonic television and video discs. Messages are coming at us and enveloping us. Most recently, the television screen has been supplemented by the omnipresent computer video display terminals, often with accompanying audio features, commonly used in business and recreation. At work and at home, dynamic visual and audio communication is the order of the day, and the end is not in sight. The video disc is not the latest device. An "AromaDisc Player," which diffuses fragrance from a disc in the same way a turntable dispenses sound from a record, is on the market. You can choose from twenty different discs providing such fragrances as "Ocean Breeze," with its seaside scent, or "Movietime," emitting the smell of popcorn.

A recently developed multi-sensory device, called the Environ, was installed in seventy health clubs and corporations in 1984. It is a human-sized, comfortably furnished cylinder that "treats" the person seated inside by illuminating the surroundings with tiny Christmas tree-type bulbs, dispensing a sweet scent of eucalyptus, and massaging the body. It is popularly called "The Bliss Machine." What more is to come? Projections are being made that we will

> become progressively less verbal, and a new cinematic or television-oriented language that is primarily visual will become our main communications medium. . . .
> . . . In this new "Computerspeak," [asserts Lee Brewer, writer and director of Mabou Mines, an avant-garde theater company in New York] pictures, visual images, and mood-altering colors rather than words and sentences will dominate communication.[1]

As a result, "man now learns, feels, and thinks differently than he did before the advent of electronic communication."[2] Marshall McLuhan pointed out that the media "work us over completely . . . [and the] medium is the massage" of several of our senses simultaneously. "Ours is a brand-new world of allatonceness."[3]

The world around us is getting in on the act. It is no accident that at the grocery store as you look at the sale signs and the attractive displays you are hearing piped-in music designed to put you in the mood to buy. Maybe you remember the last time you entered a department store and were surrounded immediately by the sight of the merchandise, the sounds of Muzak or music produced by Audio Environments, Inc., and the fragrance of the perfume counter. Or, do you remember opening your newspaper or magazine to a scented page with an ad announcing a new fragrance in perfume?

We seem nearly to have arrived in the "brave new world" of the "synthetic-talking, coloured, stereo-scopic Feely [instead of "movie"] with Synchronized Scent-Organ Accompaniment" envisioned by Aldous Huxley in 1932.

Should Preaching Incorporate Video Technology?

This multisensory orientation of our society presents a pressure point for contemporary preaching. The same people who are getting their news visually from a television set at 6:00 P.M. are receiving your message at 11:00 A.M. Sunday by exclusively oral communication. What is the best response to the situation? Obviously, the use of vivid, sensory language in every sermon is essential. It is possible to evoke an image on the screen of the listener's mind. But beyond that, what? Should preaching incorporate video technology?

Michael Bell boldly advocates radical revision, believing that preaching "is left with an option. It can try and compete with these environments, and if it does so it will surely die, or it can find its role within and become part of this new explosion"[4] of mass media communications. Achtemeier is more cautious but muses: "It may be that our age, so accustomed to the visual and sensual, needs new forms to overcome its dullness of hearing and obdurancy [*sic*] of heart."[5]

It might be helpful to listen to Bettinghaus, a specialist in communication theory. Regarding multiple communication channels, he says, "there are many situations in which the use of two sense modalities will provide a distinct service to the communicator in improving his chances of making an effective presentation to an audience." If the content of the material is complementary, not contradictory, and the presentation is deliberately paced, not too fast, multiple channel communication can be helpful in gaining initial attention, maintaining attention during long presentations, clarifying complex content, or emphasizing one part of a message.[6]

Perhaps that explains the fact that in a Mobil Oil Co. experiment in communication, after three days "only 10% of the material taught by simple telling could be recalled, 20% of the material was recalled which had been only shown, while 65% of the material taught by both telling and showing was recalled."[7]

Media Doesn't Displace the Minister

Such data may indicate, as Lyle Schaller said, that "one ingredient of effective preaching is visual communication that may call for supplementing [the sermon] with slides and audio-visual materials."[8] There is no validity in the minister being displaced by media, but it may be valid to use an occasional media-augmented message. This concept veers away from the traditional church sermon. But there is no reason why the enhanced effectiveness visual communication has enjoyed in industrial and educational settings cannot also be used, from time to time, in church.

Thor Hall, a strong advocate of the use of visual media in preaching, is correct, however, in warning against a complete sell-out to visual communication. "For better or for worse, preaching is an oral medium. . . . If a preacher isn't able to communicate freely and openly with his people through the most personal medium of all—his own voice, words, and body—there is really no reason to hope that he will reach any degree of immediacy and authenticity by surrounding himself with a whole battery of secondary, technical media."[9]

Some large churches, of course, can afford expensive technology and equipment. Churches recently constructed often have multiple microphone jacks at strategic places around the platform area. They also may be equipped with rear-screen projection so that slides or an outline or a map may be incorporated into the message without interrupting the service. Multiple projectors, carefully synchronized to change the imagery on the screen, can be computer-controlled to suit your needs.

Media augmentation can occur, however, in the simplest of settings. All you need is a good camera, a home slide projector, and a screen. Someone can help you operate the simple home slide projector, changing the picture at certain cues you provide.

Perhaps a suggestion will illustrate the point. The passage of Scripture in Luke 12:13–21 deals with the man who came asking Jesus to be a judge and divider over his family estate. Jesus detected that the man was covetous and told the parable about the rich man building bigger barns. During the reading of the Scripture introducing the sermon, someone could project slides depicting bumper crops and full barns in such a way that they correlate with the reading of the text. Then, point out that greed is just as prevalent in our twentieth-century industrial, commercial, and technological society as in the first-century's agrarian society. Retell the parable in a contemporary, commercial setting. As you do, project slides showing what tempts us to be greedy today. These slides could portray a copy of a will, a safe deposit box that is full, stock portfolios that are stuffed, or any other symptom of contemporary covetousness. After the introduction portraying first- and twentieth-century greed, you could terminate the projection and move into the body of the sermon. An outline of this would be as follows, with you saying:

A United Press International release tells of the Treasure Salvors Incorporated attempt to try to raise treasure from the galleon *Nuestra Senora De Atocha*, which sank in a 1622 hurricane about 40 miles west of Key West, Florida. The firm had converted a tug boat into a salvage ship and was attempting to recover an estimated 100 million dollar treasure from the sunken ship.

During one night, the north wind rolled the ship on its side at anchor before dawn, pitching 13 crewmen into the Gulf of Mexico. Three people were trapped below decks. They were the captain of the ship, his wife, and a salvage diver. They drowned trying to get rich.[10]

They were not the only people running the risk of dying trying to get rich. Greed can be a destructive thing.

That is what Jesus was pointing out in a story he told. A man came to him asking him to be arbiter, an executor of the family's estate. Jesus responded by saying that he did not come to do that kind of thing:

slide of a crop ready for harvest	16. And He told them a parable, saying, "The land of a certain rich man was very productive.
slide of a barn	17. "And he began reasoning to himself, saying, 'What shall I do since I have no place to store my crops?'
slide of a larger barn or several barns	18. "and he said, 'This is what I will do: I will tear down my barns and build larger ones, and there I will store all my grain and my goods.

19. 'And I will say to my soul, "Soul, you have many goods laid up for many years to come; take your ease, eat, drink and be merry." '

20. "But God said to him, 'You fool! This very night your soul is required of you; and now who will own what you have prepared?'

21. "So is the man who lays up treasure for himself, and is not rich toward God."

By this story Jesus pointed out the destructive nature of human greed. Human nature doesn't change, and there are people today just like the man in the story. If Jesus were living in our day he probably would say something like this to many of us:

slide of stock certificates or bonds

16. The investments of a very rich man yielded large dividends and capital gains.

slides of a bank and a safe deposit box

17. And he said to himself, "What shall I do, to tax shelter some of my income since I'm already in the 50 percent tax bracket?"

slide of an IRS 1040 form

18. And he said, "This is what I will do: I will buy tax-free municipal bonds and I will rollover my individual retirement account.

slide of a hospital
coronary care unit sign

19. Then I'll be able to take it easy and have a good time, knowing that there is no way that inflation could erode my security for the future."

20. But God said to him, "You fool! Tonight you're going to have a heart attack; then who will own what you have?"

21. It's a destructive thing to be greedy instead of godly.

Recasting the parable in terms of our contemporary culture and augmenting that by contemporary communication techniques (visual projection) can help make the truth of the parable sound and feel relevant to modern life. When the oral presentation of both parables, accompanied by the visual presentations, has been completed, you simply terminate the imagery projection and go on to the body of the message. Of course, it is possible that projection could be used during the sermon also. However, too much of this might be distracting.

17

Three Variations in Preaching

TRADITIONAL BIBLICAL SERMONS are usually deductive in structure. The sermon begins with a text that (hopefully) is exegeted accurately and explained. It then moves toward the application of the truths of the text to the lives of the hearers. Then it may or may not be illustrated. But the beginning point is the text, and only after that is explained does the sermon deal with contemporary life.

The Inductive Message

Because the modern mind typically thinks inductively, it is sometimes helpful to reverse that pattern and use an inductive approach to the sermon. The advent of the modern scientific method has oriented people toward inductive patterns of thought. In science this method takes the pattern of gathering data, assimilating it, analyzing it, and moving toward a general truth that explains it. Sermons can be constructed that way also. It is possible in preaching to begin with the data and experiences of life and move toward Scripture. This will not make the sermon any less biblical. As long as the sermon is in touch with both the Bible and life, it is a biblical sermon.

171

Basically, then, the inductive sermon structure in its simplest form is actually a one-point sermon in reverse. You don't begin with the text. You begin with life. You move through situations or problems of life, and perhaps illustrations of them, toward the text. There are no points in this type of sermon structure. Most of the time a formal introduction isn't necessary, particularly if the sermon begins with a concrete life situation or problem (or an illustration of one). You don't need a traditional conclusion because the text is announced and explained as the point toward which the whole sermon has moved. The inductive technique is like a nominating speech in which all of the content is stated in such a way that, by the time the speaker arrives at the point of announcing the nominee, the listener already knows who it is. In the inductive sermon, by the time the text is introduced and explained, the thrust of the message has already become increasingly clear. The sharing of the text and the explanation of it serve to validate and authenticate the truth.

Don't treat the text lightly when you arrive at it. It should not be a Scripture having only a casual connection with the message, but one which, properly interpreted, does indeed relate to the prior sermon material. It "should not be a mere appendix or addendum for the sake of biblical sanction, but should be a vital part of the sermon and its inductive movement."[11]

Although the sermon won't have points because it has only one point (the central truth of the text), it will need structure so that the preacher can learn the message and make it flow progressively toward its goal. Movement, not points as such, provides the structure of the message. Two particular types of message are naturally conveyed by this sermonic form.

Movement Toward the Text as the Solution of a Problem

The sermon can begin with a problem or situation in life and pursue a biblical solution or approach to that problem.

The use of this method is particularly helpful in efforts at "life situation" preaching. The following suggested structure will provide the flow toward the biblical answer.

1. You are "here" (the statement of the problem).

2. How did you get here? (the origin or development of the problem).

3. What's it like to be here? (the emotional, social, and other complexities of the problem).

4. Has anybody else ever been here? (the prevalence of the problem in contemporary life, in historical characters, and/or biblical characters).

5. What if you don't get out of here? (the consequences of the problem).

6. How *could* you get out of here? (the alternative solutions to the problem, perhaps including pros and cons of each).

7. What's the *best* way out of here? (a biblical solution as seen in a biblical character who effectively dealt with a similar problem, or a biblical statement that provides direction in dealing with the problem).[12]

Movement Toward the Text as a Biblical Principle

The basically inductive approach can be used in a message other than a "problem solving" message. In the first segment of this type of message, you observe life, noticing a recurring truth or principle. In the second phase, you articulate and clarify the principle. In the last phase of the message, you share a biblical text that affirms that principle. Dwight Stevenson provided in *The Biblical Preacher's Workshop* a sermon entitled "Reaping More Than We Sow" which illustrates this method. The sermon begins with a series of illustrations from various areas of life that suggest that people receive much more in life than they deserve. This idea is then observed as true in most human relationships. Finally, it is seen with respect to the relationship to God, as delineated in Ephesians 2:8. The text is, at the end of the sermon, quoted and briefly emphasized and explained.[13] Those wanting to explore the whole range of inductive preaching techniques more thoroughly will find help available.[14]

The Segmented Sermon

Another novel technique in preaching involves the division of the sermon into segments, each of which is presented alternately with another element of worship. Carefully selected components of worship are interspersed between the parts of the sermon. The end result is that the minister does not speak long at any one time, but the total preaching time may equal or exceed that of the normal sermon.

The relatively brief time that the worshiper is expected to focus on any one thing is one advantage of the segmental sermon. John Stacey observed that "two of the most influential places in our society are the television studio and the classroom, and in neither of those two places would anyone in his right mind dream of standing up and talking for twenty minutes without stopping."[15] The hearer's attention span is rather short. If you as a preacher are not sympathetic with that, make it a point to notice how many times your thoughts begin to wander the next time you listen to a thirty-minute sermon. Or, just sit in your easy chair for thirty minutes and feel how long that is! Imagine how much a person ought to be able to say in that amount of time.

Modern media have taken into consideration the relatively brief attention span of most listeners. One of the guidelines in television newscasting is that the stories presented should be brief, normally no more than two minutes long. Any segment longer than that, it is said, leaves the viewer bored.

The average listener is programmed for a fast-paced world. He or she has a hard time concentrating on one speaker for any length of time. If you can provide some break in the presentation and some movement, the attention usually is held more effectively.

Another advantage of the segmented sermon lies in the possibility of enhancing the impact of particular parts of the message by inserting some other element of worship complementary to that part of the message. Too often in the traditional sermon the impact of what you say is diminished because it is followed by more words. The use of other more emotive and interesting features can heighten the force of what has just been said.

Besides that, the segmented sermon can be used to produce a more cohesive worship service than most people normally experience. In far too many experiences of worship, the focus of the worshiper's attention is fragmented. The music is often on one subject, the message on another. Planning the other components of worship around the theme of the message will help produce a unified worship experience. Of course, for that tō ʰe true each component must be carefully selected to insure that its subject matter is consistent with the part of the sermon it is inserted into, and it must be strategically placed next to the part of the sermon it complements.

But what nonsermonic features can be incorporated into the presentation of the message? Various options are available.

Scripture readings are an obvious possibility. Responsive readings of Scripture involving the congregation can be used alternately with segments of the message. This will have the effect of drawing the hearer in to the message, making him or her a part of the preaching event, and providing a dialogical effect. Antiphonal readings involving choir groups can also be very effective.

Music in various forms—congregational singing, a choral presentation, a solo, or instrumental music—can also be effective in complementing a segment of a message.[16] Too often, preachers simply quote the words of a familiar hymn as an illustrative element in a sermon. Ordinarily that does not have much impact. A more effective approach would be for the congregation to join in singing the words in order to experience the poignancy of the text of the hymn and its relationship to that part of the message. If the congregation cannot sing the hymn, the choir could present it at the appropriate time. After the hymn has been sung, you then proceed to the next segment of your message.

For example, during a sermon about the love of God, you could develop the point that the love of God is enduring. As you develop the point, you might illustrate it by sharing the circumstances behind the writing of the the hymn "O Love That Will Not Let Me Go." The hymn was written by George Matheson of Glasgow, Scotland. While engaged to be married, he became ill. The diagnosis was partial blindness, and the prognosis was total blindness. At that point, his fiancée broke the engagement because she did not want to love a blind man all of her life. Out of that bitter disappointment, George Matheson wrote the hymn, contrasting human love—so fragile and easily broken—with divine love which is durable.

At this point in your message, by prior arrangement with the minister of music and, perhaps, instruction to the congregation before the preaching has begun, the worshipers could sing the hymn, or the choir could present it. This kind of illustrative material concerning the background of hymns can be found in *Hymns of Our Faith*,[17] a book that provides background information on 554 hymns and tunes with biographical material on authors and composers, with special attention given to the circumstances behind the composition of each hymn.

The Drama-Augmented Sermon

In the same way that you can develop a media-augmented message, you can also provide a dramatic presentation accompanying one segment of a sermon. For example, Luke 18:9–14 records the story of the Pharisees and the publican. While the text is being read from the pulpit or from a microphone somewhere else in the sanctuary, a group of people dressed in the garb of Bible times could act out a brief drama on one side of the pulpit. To show that pride is not only the plague of first-century people, but of us as well, on the other side of the pulpit another group in modern dress could display the same moods and temperaments of the Pharisees and the publican. Following the brief dramatic presentation, you could move into the presentation of the body of the message.

Suggestions made here certainly don't exhaust the possibilities. They are intended simply to spark your imagination and creativity. You know your congregation, and you can invent and experiment with a vast array of innovative approaches with which you and your congregation will be comfortable.

18

Some Words of Advice

BEFORE YOU TRY IT. . . . The old adage "be not the first by which the new is tried—be not the last to lay the old aside" is almost unconsciously or subconsciously the rule by which many preachers live. In the relatively insecure profession of ministry, many find a sense of security in perpetuating a middle of the road sameness. But you may have to forget the first part of that old adage. You very well may be the first in the community or congregation you serve to try some of these new forms. Don't be afraid. The validity of biblical preaching is not determined by its form. But before you try new forms, several suggestions may help make it a pleasant and productive experience for you and your congregation.

Don't let down your hermeneutical guard in the effort to be avant-garde. Be sure not to let your eagerness for creativity and innovation lead you into faulty hermeneutics. No matter how interesting your product may be, it will not be a biblical message if it does not interpret accurately the Scripture it deals with.

Choose the new forms that you can be relatively

comfortable with. Not all preachers will be able to use all the innovative forms easily. The congregation will certainly be paying attention to you more closely than usual. If you are uncomfortable, your uneasiness will create anxiety and nervousness in your hearers. No one wants a catastrophe to occur (they are as concerned about that as you are), so use the variations of sermon form and innovative techniques that you can handle naturally. You will have to assess your own abilities and orientations and choose wisely. Perhaps enough suggestions have been made to enable you to find the ones which you can use. A "cafeteria" approach has been followed—many options have been laid out. Go through and pick out what you will—and what your congregation will let you.

Select the form of sermon that fits the content of the sermon. Some methods are a better "fit" for certain subjects or certain texts. You will want to give some attention to matching the form with the message and/or text.

Begin in the least conspicuous way, and become comfortable with small changes. Try an innovative segment in a traditional sermon. After having become acquainted with the different devices of experimental preaching, you can insert one of these as an experimental factor in a traditional sermon.

Let your first experimental sermon be one of the more simple forms, and do it in the smallest setting in the church. Don't tackle the complex at the eleven o'clock hour of worship on Sunday morning. The mid-week service, a Sunday evening service, or a special occasion for speaking to the congregation provide a better setting for your first use of an experimental form.

Prepare your people for any major departures from the normal. Don't surprise people with an unexpected radical departure from traditional methods since, as John Stacey said, "people tend to resent 'having things sprung on them.' "[18] Achtemeier agrees that "there must be some understanding and expectation of experimental forms created in the congregation before those forms can be used with any effectiveness whatsoever. Otherwise, the members of the church are alienated."[19]

Anticipate the effect any changes you make may have upon others who are a part of the leadership in worship. If the procedure of your experimental message is going to have some impact on the ushers, the operator of the sound system and lights, the minister of music, or the instrumentalists, you need to acquaint them fully with what you are going to do and its impact on them.

Tailor the delivery style to fit the innovative technique chosen. Eliminate any clergy or ministerial artifices in your delivery. Be sure to avoid a ministerial tone in these forms of sermons. Such artifices should never occur in any kind of sermon, but they must be avoided like the plague in the newer forms.

Maintain your focus on effective communication of the gospel. "Many self-styled avant-garde preachers become so enamored with gimmicks and gadgetry that their presentations tend to be 'Productions' or 'Specials' more than genuine sermons."[20]

Feel the pulsebeat of the congregation and move at their pace. Some congregations are by nature progressive and creative in all areas of their fellowship. In these situations, the innovative preaching forms may need to be used frequently, with an occasional reversion to the basic forms. Most congregations, however, are by nature conservative. Avoid the temptation of putting such a congregation into shock. You will need to establish yourself in a church, assure the people that you are committed to the preservation of those values in the past that are legitimate, and convince them of your commitment to the basic Christian faith before using innovative forms of the sermon. As they begin to get used to it, you can increase the frequency of the use of innovative sermon forms. Even then, you will need to temper experimental preaching with consideration for those who prefer the traditional forms.

The suggestions shared about innovative preaching forms are, of course, suggestive, not exhaustive. It is hoped that they will serve as catalysts for new ideas of your own about how to achieve variety in biblical preaching—how to offer the "bread of life" in new loaves (shapes) and to put "the old wine in new wineskins."

Bibliography

Books

Abelson, Herbert I. *Persuasion: How Opinions and Attitudes Are Changed*. New York: Springer Publishing Company, 1959.

Achtemeier, Elizabeth. *Creative Preaching: Finding the Words*. Nashville: Abingdon Press, 1980.

Augustine. *On Christian Doctrine*. 4. 2–3.

Bailey, Lloyd R. *The Pentateuch*. Interpreting Biblical Texts Series. Nashville: Abingdon Press, 1981.

Barclay, William. *The Master's Men*. Nashville: Abingdon Press, 1969.

Barton, John. *Reading the Old Testament: Method in Biblical Study*. Philadelphia: The Westminster Press, 1984.

Baumann, Daniel. *An Introduction to Preaching*. Grand Rapids: Baker Book House, 1972.

Beekman, John, and Callow, John. *Translating the Word of God*. Grand Rapids: Zondervan, 1974.

Best, Ernest. *From Text to Sermon: Responsible Use of the New Testament in Preaching*. Atlanta: John Knox Press, 1978.

Bettinghaus, Erwin P. *Persuasive Communication*. 2nd ed. New York: Holt, Rinehart and Winston, 1973.

Bohren, Rudolph. *Preaching and Community*. Translated by David E. Green. Richmond, Va.: John Knox Press, 1965.

Bradley, Bert E. *Fundamentals of Speech Communication: The Credibility of Ideas*. Dubuque, Ia.: William C. Brown Publishing Company, 1974.

Brehm, J. W., and Cohen, A. R. *Explorations in Cognitive Dissonance*. New York: Wiley, 1962.

Brown, H. C., Jr.; Clinard, H. Gordon; and Northcutt, Jesse J. *Steps to the Sermon*. Nashville: Broadman Press, 1963.

Buber, Martin. *Between Man and Man*. Translated by Ronald Gregor Smith. London: Routledge and Kegan Paul, 1947.

Buechner, Frederick. *Peculiar Treasures: A Biblical Who's Who*. San Francisco: Harper and Row, 1979.

———. *Telling the Truth: The Gospel as Tragedy, Comedy, and Fairy Tale*. New York: Harper and Row, 1977.

Calloud, Jean. *Structural Analysis of Narrative*. Translated by Daniel Patte. Philadelphia: Fortress Press, 1976.

Childs, Brevard S. *Introduction to the Old Testament as Scripture*. Philadelphia: Fortress Press, 1979.

Cox, James W., ed. *Biblical Preaching: An Expositor's Treasury*. Philadelphia: The Westminster Press, 1983.

Craddock, Fred B. *As One Without Authority*. 3rd ed. Nashville: Abingdon, 1979.

———. *Overhearing the Gospel*. Nashville: Abingdon, 1978.

Crossan, John D. *In Parables: The Challenges of the Historical Jesus*. 1st ed. New York: Harper and Row, 1973.

Davis, H. Grady. *Design for Preaching*. Philadelphia: Fortress Press, 1958.

Deen, Edith. *All the Women of the Bible*. New York: Harper and Brothers, 1955.

Dodd, C. H. *The Parables of the Kingdom*, Rev. ed. New York: Scribner's, 1961.

Douglas, Lloyd C. *The Robe*. Boston: Houghton-Mifflin Co., 1969.

Fant, Clyde E. *Preaching for Today*. New York: Harper and Row, 1975.

Forsyth, P. T. *Positive Preaching and the Modern Mind*. New York: George H. Doran, 1907.

Hall, Thor. *The Future Shape of Preaching*. Philadelphia: Fortress Press, 1971.

Harrison, Everett. *Jesus and His Contemporaries*. Grand Rapids: Baker Book House, 1970.

Hoefler, Richard Carl. *Creative Preaching and Oral Writing*. Lima, Ohio: The C.S.S. Publishing Co., 1978.

Hovland, Carl I.; Janis, Irving L.; and Kelley, Harold H. *Communication and Persuasion*. New Haven: Yale University Press, 1953.

Howe, Reuel. *Partners in Preaching: Clergy and Laity in Dialogue*. New York: The Seabury Press, 1967.

Hubbard, David Allen. *They Met Jesus.* Philadelphia: A. J. Holman Company, 1974.

Hull, William E. "Preaching on the Synoptic Gospels." In *Biblical Preaching: An Expositor's Treasury,* pp. 169–94. Edited by James W. Cox. Philadelphia: The Westminster Press, 1983.

Huxley, Aldous. *Brave New World.* New York: Harper and Brothers, 1932.

Jensen, Richard A. *Telling the Story.* Minneapolis: Augsburg Publishing House, 1980.

Jeremias, Joachim. *The Parables of Jesus.* Translated by S. H. Hooks. Rev. ed. New York: Scribner's, 1963.

Jones, Ilion T. *Principles and Practice of Preaching.* New York: Abingdon Press, 1956.

Jones, Peter Rhea. *The Teaching of the Parables.* Nashville: Broadman Press, 1982.

Kambler, Howard. *Communication: Sharing Our Stories of Experience.* Seattle: Psychological Press, 1983.

Kierkegaard, Søren. *Purity of Heart Is to Will One Thing.* Translated by Douglas V. Steere. Rev. ed. New York: Harper and Brothers, 1948.

Killinger, John. *Leave It to the Spirit.* New York: Harper and Row, 1971.

———. "The New Shape of Preaching." In *Contemporary Christian Trends,* pp. 27–38. Edited by William M. Pinson, Jr. and Clyde E. Fant, Jr. Waco, Tex.: Word Books, 1972.

Lewis, Ralph L. with Lewis, Gregg. *Inductive Preaching: Helping People Listen.* Westchester, Ill.: Crossway Books, 1983.

Lewis, Sinclair. *Elmer Gantry.* New York: The New American Library, Inc., Signet Classics, 1967.

Lowry, Eugene L. *Doing Time in the Pulpit: The Relationship Between Narrative and Preaching.* Nashville: Abingdon Press, 1985.

———. *The Homiletical Plot: The Sermon as Narrative Art Form.* Atlanta: John Knox Press, 1980.

Macartney, Clarence E. *Chariots of Fire and Other Sermons on Bible Characters.* New York: Abingdon Press, 1951.

———. *Sermons on Old Testament Heroes.* Nashville: Cokesbury Press, 1935.

McEachern, Alton. *Dramatic Monologue Preaching*. Nashville: Broadman Press, 1984.

McLuhan, Marshall. *Understanding the Media*. New York: McGraw-Hill Book Company, 1964.

McLuhan, Marshall, and Fiore, Quentin. *The Medium Is the Massage*. New York: Random House, Inc., 1967.

Marshall, I. Howard, ed. *New Testament Interpretation: Essays on Principles and Methods*. Grand Rapids: William B. Eerdmans Publishing Company, 1977.

Miller, Donald G. *Fire in Thy Mouth*. New York: Abingdon Press, 1954.

Mitchell, Henry H. *The Recovery of Preaching*. Harper's Minister's Paperback Library. San Francisco: Harper and Row, 1977.

Moore, George Foot. *Judaism*. Vol. 1. Cambridge: Harvard University Press, 1927.

Newton, Joseph Fort. *The New Preaching*. Nashville: Cokesbury Press, 1930.

Nida, Eugene A., and Taber, Charles R. *The Theory and Practice of Translation*. Leiden: United Bible Societies, 1974.

Oursler, Fulton. *The Greatest Faith Ever Known*. New York: Doubleday and Company, Inc., 1953.

Patte, Daniel. *What Is Structural Exegesis?* Philadelphia: Fortress Press, 1976.

Perry, Lloyd M. *Biblical Preaching for Today's World*. Chicago: Moody Press, 1973.

————. *Biblical Sermon Guide*. Grand Rapids: Baker Book House, 1970.

Polzin, Robert M. *Biblical Structuralism: Method and Subjectivity in the Study of Ancient Texts*. Philadelphia: Fortress Press, 1977.

Randolph, David James. *The Renewal of Preaching*. Philadelphia: Fortress Press, 1969.

Reid, Clyde H. *The Empty Pulpit*. New York: Harper and Row, 1967.

Reynolds, William Jensen, ed. *Hymns of Our Faith*. Nashville: Broadman Press, 1964.

Rice, Charles. "Shaping Sermons by the Interplay of the Text and Metaphor." In *Preaching Biblically*, pp. 101–11. Edited by Don M. Wardlaw. Philadelphia: The Westminster Press, 1983.

Safrai, S., and Stern, M., in cooperation with Flusser, D., and Van Unnik, W. C. *The Jewish People in the First Century: Historical Geography, Political History, Social, Cultural and Religious Life and Thought*. Section One, Vols. I and II in the *Compendia Rerum Iudaicarum ad Novum Testamentum*. Philadelphia: Fortress Press, 1974 [Vol. I] and 1976 [Vol. II].

Sherif, Carolyn W.; Sherif, Muzafer; and Nebergall, Roger. *Attitude and Attitude Change: The Social Judgment-Involvement Approach*. Philadelphia: W. B. Saunders Company, 1965.

Skelton, Eugene. *Meet the Prophets*. Nashville: Broadman Press, 1972.

Speakman, Frederick W. *The Salty Tang*. Westwood, N. J.: Fleming H. Revell Co., 1954.

———. "What Pilate Said One Midnight." In *The Twentieth-Century Pulpit*, Vol. 1, pp. 214–19. Edited by James W. Cox. Nashville: Abingdon, 1978.

Steimle, Edmund A.; Niedenthal, Morris J.; Rice, Charles R. *Preaching the Story*. Philadelphia: Fortress Press, 1980.

Steinsaltz, Adin. *Biblical Images*. New York: Basic Books, Inc., 1984.

Stevenson, Dwight E. *In the Biblical Preacher's Workshop*. Nashville: Abingdon Press, 1967.

Stone, Michael E. *Jewish Writings of the Second Temple Period: Apocrypha, Pseudepigrapha, Qumran Sectarian Writings, Philo, Josephus*. Section Two, Vol. II in the *Compendia Rerum Iudaicarum ad Novum Testamentum*. Philadelphia: Fortress Press, 1984.

Stott, John R. W. *Between Two Worlds*. Grand Rapids: William B. Eerdmans Publishing Company, 1982.

———. *The Preacher's Portrait in the New Testament*. Grand Rapids: William B. Eerdmans Publishing Company, 1961.

Swank, George. *Dialogic Style in Preaching*. The More Effective Preaching Series. Valley Forge, Pa.: Judson Press, 1981.

Thielicke, Helmut. *The Waiting Father*. Translated by John W. Doberstein. New York: Harper and Row, 1959.

Thompson, Wayne N. *Fundamentals of Communication*. New York: McGraw-Hill, 1957.

Thompson, William D., and Bennett, Gordon C. *Dialogue Preaching*. Valley Forge, Pa.: Judson Press, 1969.

Toffler, Alvin. *Future Shock.* New York: Random House, 1970.

Via, D. O., Jr. *The Parables: Their Literary and Existential Dimension.* Philadelphia: Fortress Press, 1967.

Wardlaw, Don M. "Introduction: The Need for New Shapes." In *Preaching Biblically,* pp. 11–25. Edited by Don M. Wardlaw. Philadelphia: The Westminster Press, 1983.

Wiesel, Elie. *Five Biblical Portraits.* London: University of Notre Dame Press, 1981.

————. *Messengers of God.* New York: Random House, 1976.

Wilder, Amos N. *The Language of the Gospel.* New York: Harper and Row, 1964.

Wright, G. Ernest. *The God Who Acts: Biblical Theology as Recital.* London: SCM Press Ltd., 1952.

Reference Works and Biblical Commentaries

Ackroyd, Peter; Barr, James; Bright, John; and Wright, G. Ernest, gen. eds. *The Old Testament Library.* Philadelphia: The Westminster Press. Various volumes available and forthcoming.

Bornkamm, Günther; Barth, Gerhard; and Held, Heinz Joachim. *Tradition and Interpretation in Matthew.* Translated by Percy Scott. In *The New Testament Library.* Philadelphia: The Westminster Press. 1963.

Burgers, W. J.; Sysling, H.; and Tomson, P. J.; gen. eds. *Compendia Rerum Iudaicarum ad Novum Testamentum.* Philadelphia: Fortress Press. Three volumes available, two forthcoming.

Conzelmann, Hanz. *The Theology of St. Luke.* Translated by Geoffrey Buswell. New York: Harper and Brothers, 1960.

Cross, Frank M., Jr., and Koester, Helmut, gen. eds. *Hermenia–A Critical and Historical Commentary of the Whole Bible.* Philadelphia: Fortress Press. Various volumes available and forthcoming.

Gasque, W. Ward, ed. *A Good News Commentary.* San Francisco: Harper and Row. Various volumes available and forthcoming.

Gove, Philip Babcock, ed. *Webster's Third New International Dictionary of the English Language, Unabridged.* Springfield, Ma.: G. and C. Merriam Co., 1961.

Gundry, Robert. *Matthew, A Commentary on His Literary and Theological Art.* Grand Rapids: William B. Eerdmans Publishing Company, 1982.

Hubbard, David A., and Barker, Glenn W., gen. eds. *Word Biblical Commentary.* Waco, Tex.: Word Publishing Company. Various volumes available and forthcoming.

Kelley, Page H. "Isaiah." In *The Broadman Bible Commentary.* Vol. 5, pp. 149–374. Edited by Clifton J. Allen. Nashville: Broadman Press, 1971.

Knight, G. A. F. *Theology as Narration: A Commentary on the Book of Exodus.* Grand Rapids: William B. Eerdmans Publishing Company, 1976.

Lane, William. *Commentary on the Gospel of Mark.* In *The New International Commentary on the New Testament.* Grand Rapids: William B. Eerdmans Publishing Company, 1974.

Marshall, I. Howard. *Gospel of Luke: A Commentary on the Greek Text.* In *The New International Greek Testament Commentary.* Grand Rapids: William B. Eerdmans Publishing Company, 1978.

Martin, Ralph. *Mark, Evangelist and Theologian.* In *Contemporary Evangelical Perspectives.* Grand Rapids: Zondervan Publishing Corporation, 1972.

Marxsen, Willi. *Mark the Evangelist: Studies on the Redaction History of the Gospel.* Translated by James Boyce, Donald Juel, William Poehlmann, with Roy A. Harrisville. Nashville: Abingdon Press, 1969.

Mays, James Luther, gen. ed. *Interpretation: A Bible Commentary on Preaching and Teaching.* Atlanta: John Knox Press. Various volumes available and forthcoming.

Periodical Articles

Achtemeier, Elizabeth. "The Artful Dialogue." *Interpretation* 35 (January 1981): 18–31.

Babin, David E. "Examining the Potentialities of Monologue Preaching." *Preaching* 5 (September-October, 1970): 24–34.

Bell, Michael. "Preaching in Our Mass Media Environment." *Preaching* 4 (January-February, 1969): 1–27.

Blair, Burton F. "Preaching as a Homiletical Plot." *Pulpit Digest* 62 (November-December, 1982): 23–25.

Brokhof, John R. "Preaching Dialogically." *Pulpit Digest* 63 (May-June, 1983): 36–38.

Cambell, Ernest T. "Who Do You Say That I Am?" *Sermons from Riverside,* no volume indicated (4 April 1976): 1–6.

Cox, James W. "Dialogue in Preaching." *Pulpit Digest* 49 (May-June 1979): 52.

Fosdick, Harry Emerson. "What Is the Matter with Preaching?" *Pulpit Digest* 63 (September-October 1983): 8–16. Reprint from *Harper's Magazine* 157 (July 1928).

Grossman, John. "You May Not Believe This One." *Geo* 5 (August, 1983): 54.

"Growth Expert Cites Development." *The Baptist Standard* (June 15, 1977): 16.

Hatch, Leonard J. "Let Your Laymen Help You Preach." *The New Pulpit Digest* 57 (November-December 1977): 27–28.

Homrighausen, Elmer G. "God's Story and Our Story: A Worship Service Based on Ephesians." *Pulpit Digest* 60 (January-February 1980): 21–23.

Hovland, Carl I. "Reconciling Conflicting Results Derived from Experimental and Survey Studies of Attitude Change." *The American Psychologist* 14 (January 1959): 8–17.

Hovland, Carl I.; Harvey, O. J.; and Sherif, Muzafer. "Assimilation and Contrast Effects in Reactions to Communication and Attitude Change." *The Journal of Abnormal and Social Psychology* 55 (September 1957): 244–52.

Hovland, Carl I., and Mandell, Wallace. "An Experimental Comparison of Conclusion-Drawing by the Communicator and by the Audiences." *The Journal of Abnormal and Social Psychology* 47 (July 1952): 581–88.

Interpretation 37 (October 1983).

Larson, Carl E. "Factors in Small Group Interaction." *Preaching* 3 (November-December 1968): 17–21.

"Letter from Arthur R. Riel, Jr." *Good News Letter* 36 (June 1982): 2.

Lischer, Richard. "The Limits of Story." *Interpretation* 38 (January 1984): 26–38.

McEachern, Alton. "Dogma Is Drama." *Proclaim* 4 (July-September 1974): 40–43.

McKinley, Robert C. "First-Person Preaching." *Proclaim* 10 (October-December 1979): 42.

Potts, Donald R. "The Dramatic Monologue Sermon: Biblical Truth in the First Person." *Proclaim* 3 (January-March): 14–20.

Rice, Charles. "The Preacher as Storyteller." *Union Seminary Quarterly Review* 31 (Spring 1976): 182–97.

Ruopp, Harold W. "Life Situation Preaching." *Christian Century Pulpit* 12 (May 1941): 116–17.

————. "Preaching to Life Situations." *Christian Century Pulpit* 6 (January 1935): 20–21.

Sedgwick, W. B. "The Origins of the Sermon." *The Hibbert Journal* 45 (January 1947): 158–64.

Stacey, John. "How Can the Local Preacher Experiment?" *Preacher's Quarterly* 15 (June 1969): 61–64.

————. "Will Preaching Go On?" *Preacher's Quarterly* 15 (December 1969): 28–31.

Tang, Emery. "Understanding the Listener as a Movie-Goer." *Preaching* 2 (September-October 1967): 28–31.

"The Coming Revolution in the World of Culture" in "What the Next 50 Years Will Bring: A Special Supplement to Mark the Golden Anniversary of U.S. News and World Report." *U.S. News and World Report* (May 9, 1983) pp. A9–A42.

"Third National Congress on the Word of God Celebrated in Atlanta." *Good News Letter* 38 (January 1983): 1–2.

Thistlethwaite, Donald L.; DeHaan, Henry; and Kamenetzky, Joseph. "The Effects of 'Directive' and 'Non Directive' Communication Procedures on Attitudes." *The Journal of Abnormal and Social Psychology* 51 (July 1955): 107–13.

Thompson, William D. "Dialogue Preaching in a Dialogue Culture." *Preaching* 5 (January-February 1970): 16–21.

Toohey, William. "Preaching in the 70s: Does It Have a Chance?" *Preaching* 5 (November-December 1970): 33–39.

Tubbs, Stewart L. "Explicit Versus Implicit Conclusions and Audience Commitment." *Speech Monographs* 35 (March 1968): 14–19.

Walster, Elaine, and Festinger, Leon. "The Effectiveness of 'Overheard' Persuasive Communications." *The Journal of Abnormal and Social Psychology* 65 (December 1962): 395–402.

Book Reviews

Gunter, Pete A. Y. Review of *Truth Imagined,* by Eric Hoffer. *Dallas Morning News*, 17 August 1983, sec. F, p. 3.
Tinkle, Lon. Review of *Simple and Direct,* by Jacques Barzun. *Dallas Morning News*, 9 May 1976, sec. G, p. 5.

Newspaper Articles

Bloom, Stephen G. "The Bliss Machine." *Dallas Morning News*, 18 June 1984, sec. C, p. 1.
"Celebrities' Faces Sell 'People,' Editors Say." *Dallas Morning News*, 18 January 1983, sec. D, pp. 1, 8.
Fort Worth Star-Telegram, 21 July 1975.
Wright, Jim. "Fortune-Telling Sells." *Dallas Morning News*, 15 May 1983, sec. G, p. 2.

Unpublished Works

Burchette, Ray. "Some Things You Never Forget." Sermon preached at the Highland Park Baptist Church of Austin, Texas, 1 April 1979.
Campbell, Maynard. "An Investigation of the Incursion of Inductive Methodology into Preaching." Ph.D. dissertation, Southwestern Baptist Theological Seminary, 1977.
Corley, Bruce. "Probes in the Lord's Will." Southwestern Baptist Theological Seminary Chapel Message, 16 November 1977.
Dickens, George Dean. "Implications of Preaching in Selected Communications Research and Experiments 1963–1973."

Th.D. dissertation, Southwestern Baptist Theological Seminary, 1974.

Flamming, James. "The Witness of Cornelius." Sermon preached at the First Baptist Church of Abilene, Texas, no date available.

The Academy of Homiletics. "Preaching and Story." Papers Presented to the Annual Meeting of the Academy of Homiletics, Princeton, New Jersey, 1979. (Mimeographed.)

Correspondence

Letter from Dr. Lee Williams, professor of speech communication and theatre arts, Southwest Texas State University, dated November 21, 1984.

Letter from Dr. Clyde Fant dated November 6, 1984.

Notes

Part One. First Things First

1. Clyde H. Reid, *The Empty Pulpit* (New York: Harper and Row, 1967), p. 105.

2. Elizabeth Achtemeier, *Creative Preaching: Finding the Words*, Abingdon Preacher's Library (Nashville: Abingdon Press, 1980), pp. 76–77.

3. John R. Brokhof, "Preaching Dialogically," *Pulpit Digest* 63 (May–June 1983): 36.

4. Clyde E. Fant, *Preaching for Today* (New York: Harper and Row, 1975), p. 110.

5. John Killinger, *Leave It to the Spirit* (New York: Harper and Row, 1971), p. xiii.

6. Charles Rice, "Shaping Sermons by the Interplay of the Text and Metaphor," in *Preaching Biblically*, ed. Wardlaw, p. 101.

7. Elizabeth Achtemeier, "The Artful Dialogue," *Interpretation* 35 (January 1981): 29.

8. W. B. Sedgwick, "The Origins of the Sermon," *The Hibbert Journal* 45 (January 1947): 162. See also pp. 158–64.

9. Ibid.

10. John R. W. Stott, *Between Two Worlds* (Grand Rapids: Willian B. Eerdmans, 1982), p. 10.

11. William Toohey, "Preaching in the 70s: Does It Have a Chance?" *Preaching* 5 (November-December 1970): 36.

12. Carl I. Hovland and Wallace Mandell, "An Experimental Comparison of Conclusion-Drawing by the Communicator and by the Audience," *The Journal of Abnormal and Social Psychology* 47 (July 1952): 581. For advocacy of and bibliography pertinent to implicit communication, see Carolyn W. Sherif, Muzafer Sherif, and Roger Nebergall, *Attitude and Attitude Change: The Social Judgment-Involvement Approach* (Philadelphia: W. B. Saunders Company, 1965), pp. 186–92, 240–41.

For advocacy of and bibliography pertinent to explicit communication, see J. W. Brehm and A. R. Cohen, *Explorations in Cognitive Dissonance* (New York: Wiley, 1962). For bibliographic help with reference to journal and periodical literature supporting both perspectives see Carl I. Hovland, O. J. Harvey, and Muzafer Sherif, "Assimilation and Contrast Effects in Reactions to Communication and Attitude Change," *The Journal of Abnormal and Social Psychology* 55 (September 1957): 244–52; and Carl I. Hovland, "Reconciling Conflicting Results Derived from Experimental and Survey Studies of Attitude Change," *The American Psychologist* 14 (January 1959): 8–17. The debate and discussion about explicit and implicit conclusion-drawing parallels Marshall McLuhan's discussion of the media, which posits that "hot media are . . . low in participation, and cool media are high in participation or completion by the audience." See Marshall McLuhan, *Understanding Media* (New York: McGraw-Hill Book Company, 1964), pp. 22–40. Anyone wanting to investigate this subject will find help in the bibliography surrounding the McLuhan concepts.

13. Hovland and Mandell, "Experimental Comparison," p. 581. These are not perspectives to which Hovland and Mandell subscribe, but which they acknowledge the existence of and upon which they designed an experiment.

14. Elaine Walster and Leon Festinger, "The Effectiveness of 'Overheard' Persuasive Communications," *The Journal of Abnormal and Social Psychology* 65 (December 1962): 395–402.

15. Carl E. Larson, "Factors in Small Group Interaction," *Preaching* 3 (November-December 1968): 19.

16. Walster and Festinger, "Effectiveness," p. 401.

17. Eunice Cooper and Helen Dinerman, "Analysis of the Film 'Don't Be a Sucker': A Study in Communication," *Public Opinion Quarterly* 15 (1951): 249 as cited by Carl I. Hovland, Irving L. Janis, and Harold H. Kelley, *Communication and Persuasion* (New Haven: Yale University Press, 1953), pp. 100–01.

18. Hovland and Mandell, "Experimental Comparison," p. 583.

19. Donald L. Thistlethwaite, Henry DeHaan, and Joseph Kamenetzky, "The Effects of 'Directive' and 'Non Directive' Communication Procedures on Attitudes," *The Journal of Abnormal and Social Psychology* 51 (July 1955): 107–13.

20. Stewart L. Tubbs, "Explicit Versus Implicit Conclusions and Audience Commitment," *Speech Monographs* 35 (March 1968): 17.

21. Bert E. Bradley, *Fundamentals of Speech Communication: The Credibility of Ideas* (Dubuque, Ia.: William C. Brown Publishing Company, 1974), pp. 92–93. See also Herbert I. Abelson, *Persuasion: How Opinions and Attitudes Are Changed* (New York: Springer Publishing Company, 1959), pp. 10–13.

22. "Letter from Arthur R. Riel, Jr., " *Good News Letter* (A publication of the Word of God Institute in Washington, D.C.) 36 (June 1982): 2.

23. "Whilst the new hermeneutic rightly faces the problem of how the interpreter may understand the text . . . more *deeply* and *creatively*, Fuchs and Ebeling are *less concerned about how he may understand it correctly.*" A. C. Thiselton, "The New Hermeneutic," in I. Howard Marshall, ed., *New Testament Interpretation: Essays on Principles and Methods*, 1st American ed. (Grand Rapids: William B. Eerdmans Publishing Company, 1977), p. 323.

24. Erwin P. Bettinghaus, *Persuasive Communication*, 2nd ed. (New York: Holt, Rinehart and Winston, 1973), p. 127.

25. For a strong advocacy of focusing on the meaning of the text at the canonical level see Brevard S. Childs, *Introduction to the Old Testament as Scripture* (Philadelphia: Fortress Press, 1979).

26. Correspondence from Dr. Lee Williams, professor of speech communication and theatre arts, Southwest Texas State University, dated November 21, 1984.

27. See Fred B. Craddock, *Overhearing the Gospel* (Nashville: Abingdon, 1978), pp. 82–90.

28. The three factors are suggested in Hovland, Janis, and Kelley, *Communication and Persuasion*, pp. 102–4.

29. This appears to be the key to understanding Craddock's advocacy of indirect methodology at times. His proposal is offered as a way to meet "the challenge of communicating with . . . minds and hearts dulled by long and repeated exposure to the words . . . of the Christian faith. . . . These listeners are my present concern, these who through old habit have already agreed in advance of hearing and therefore do not hear." *Overhearing*, pp. 37–38. He offers the indirect method as a way for them to have a fresh hearing.

30. David James Randolph, *The Renewal of Preaching* (Philadelphia: Fortress Press, 1969), p. 89.

31. Rudolph Bohren, *Preaching and Community*, trans. by David E. Green (Richmond, Va.: John Knox Press, 1965), p. 83.

32. Ibid., p. 94.

33. Ibid., p. 86.

34. Ibid., pp. 86–87.

35. Ernest Best, *From Text to Sermon: Responsible Use of the New Testament in Preaching* (Atlanta: John Knox Press, 1978), p. 88.

Part Two   The Dramatic Monologue Message

1. "Celebrities' Faces Sell 'People,' Editors Say," *Dallas Morning News*, 18 January 1983, sec. D, p. 8.

2. Dorothy Sayers, *The Greatest Drama Ever Staged* (London: Hodder and Stoughton, 1938), p. 17, quoted in Alton McEachern, *Dramatic Monologue Preaching* (Nashville: Broadman Press, 1984), p. 11.

3. More will be said about this later, in the discussion of the media-augmented message. See pp. 163–70.

4. Alton McEachern, "Dogma Is Drama," *Proclaim* 4 (July-September 1974): 40.

5. Pete A. Y. Gunter, review of *Truth Imagined*, by Eric Hoffer, in *Dallas Morning News*, 17 August 1983, sec. F, p. 3.

6. Donald R. Potts, "The Dramatic Monologue Sermon: Biblical Truth in the First Person," *Proclaim* 3 (January-March 1973): 15.

7. McEachern, *Dramatic Monologue Preaching*, pp. 12–13.

8. McEachern, "Dogma Is Drama," p. 42.

9. Achtemeier, *Creative Preaching*, p. 82.

10. See, for example, Clarence E. Macartney, *Chariots of Fire and Other Sermons on Bible Characters* (New York: Abingdon Press, 1951); and *Sermons on Old Testament Heroes* (Nashville: Cokesbury Press, 1935). Macartney was the most prolific producer of volumes of biographical sermons in the twentieth century, some of which are available in most theological libraries.

11. Elie Wiesel, *Messengers of God* (New York: Random House, 1976); Elie Wiesel, *Five Biblical Portraits* (London: University of Notre Dame Press, 1981); Frederick Buechner, *Peculiar Treasures: A Biblical Who's Who* (San Francisco: Harper and Row, 1979); Everett F. Harrison, *Jesus and His Contemporaries* (Grand Rapids: Baker Book House, 1970); William Barclay, *The Master's Men* (Nashville: Abingdon Press, 1969); Edith Deen, *All the Women of the Bible* (New York: Harper and Brothers, 1955); Adin Steinsaltz, *Biblical Images* (New York: Basic Books, Inc., 1984).

12. Fulton Oursler, *The Greatest Faith Ever Known* (New York: Doubleday and Company, Inc., 1953); Lloyd C. Douglas, *The Robe* (Boston: Houghton-Mifflin Co., 1969). Frank Slaughter has been one of the most prolific writers in this category, with works too numerous to list. His work evidences excellent research.

13. Achtemeier, *Creative Preaching*, p. 81.

14. Achtemeier, "The Artful Dialogue," p. 29.

15. James Flamming, "The Witness of Cornelius," sermon preached at the First Baptist Church of Abilene, Texas, no date available, p. 8.

16. Ray Burchette, "Some Things You Never Forget," sermon preached at the Highland Park Baptist Church of Austin, Texas, 1 April 1979, p. 6.

17. McEachern, *Dramatic Monologue Preaching*, pp. 17–18.

18. Ernest T. Campbell, "Who Do You Say That I Am?" *Sermons from Riverside,* no volume indicated (4 April 1976): 5–6.

19. Frederick B. Speakman, *The Salty Tang* (Old Tappan, N.J.: Fleming H. Revell Co., 1954), pp. 129–30.

20. Information concerning this and other similar incidents can be found in the works of Philo, Josephus, and similar sources. It is also available in most Bible encyclopedias and dictionaries as you consult articles about biblical characters.

Especially helpful are recent releases. See Safrai, S. and Stern, M. in cooperation with Flusser, D., and Van Unnik, W. C., eds., *The Jewish People in the First Century: Historical Geography, Political History, Social, Cultural and Religious Life and Thought.* Section One, Vols. I and II of the *Compendia Rerum Iudaicarum ad Novum Testamentum* (Philadelphia: Fortress Press, 1974 [Vol. I] and 1976 [Vol. II]).

See also Stone, Michael E., ed., *Jewish Writings of the Second Temple Period: Apocrypha, Pseudepigrapha, Qumran Sectarian Writings, Philo, Josephus*, Section Two, Vol. II in the *Compendia* (Philadelphia: Fortress Press, 1984).

21. See H. Grady Davis, *Design for Preaching* (Philadelphia: Fortress Press, 1958), pp. 265–94; Wayne N. Thompson, *Fundamentals of Communication* (New York: McGraw-Hill, 1957), pp. 207–08; and Richard Carl Hoefler, *Creative Preaching and Oral Writing* (Lima, Oh.: The C. S. S. Publishing Co., 1978).

22. Correspondence from Clyde Fant, November 6, 1984. I am indebted to him for this warning and the suggestion of the alternate technique.

23. Craddock, *Overhearing*, p. 125.

24. See Frederick W. Speakman, "What Pilate Said One Midnight," in *The Twentieth-Century Pulpit*, Vol. 1, ed. James W. Cox (Nashville: Abingdon, 1978), pp. 214–19; David Allen Hubbard, *They Met Jesus* (Philadelphia: A. J. Holman Company, 1974); Eugene Skelton, *Meet the Prophets* (Nashville: Broadman Press, 1972); and McEachern, *Dramatic Monologue Preaching*.

Part Three   The Dialogical Message

1. The sporadic use of dialogical techniques in the history of preaching has been delineated in William D. Thompson and Gordon C. Bennett, *Dialogue Preaching* (Valley Forge, Pa.: Judson Press, 1969), pp. 15–23.

2. Sinclair Lewis, *Elmer Gantry* (New York: The New American Library, Inc., Signet Classics, 1967), p. 56.

3. Bettinghaus, *Persuasive Communication*, p. 11.

4. Martin Buber, *Between Man and Man*, trans., Ronald Gregor Smith (London: Routledge and Kegan Paul, 1947), p. 19.

5. Reid, *The Empty Pulpit*, p. 46.

6. Ibid., p. 78.

7. "The Coming Revolution in the World of Culture" in "A Special Supplement to Mark the Golden Anniversary of U.S. News and World Report," *U.S. News and World Report* 94 (May 9, 1983): A9.

8. Jim Wright, "Fortune-Telling Sells," *Dallas Morning News*, 15 May 1983, sec. G, p. 2.

9. William D. Thompson, "Dialogue Preaching in a Dialogue Culture," *Preaching* 5 (January-February 1970): 20.

10. P. T. Forsyth, *Positive Preaching and the Modern Mind* (New York: George H. Doran, 1907), p. 79.

11. Craddock, *Without Authority,* p. 60.

12. Forsyth, *Positive Preaching,* p. 5.

13. H. C. Brown, Jr., H. Gordon Clinard, and Jesse J. Northcutt, *Steps to the Sermon* (Nashville: Broadman Press, 1963), p. 6.

14. Donald G. Miller, *Fire in Thy Mouth* (New York: Abingdon Press, 1954), p. 17.

15. John R. W. Stott, *The Preacher's Portrait in the New Testament* (Grand Rapids: Wm. B. Eerdmans Publishing Co., 1961), pp. 52–53.

16. Fant, *Preaching for Today,* p. 29.

17. Søren Kierkegaard, *Purity of Heart Is to Will One Thing,* Rev. ed., trans Douglas V. Steere (New York: Harper and Brothers Publishers, 1948), pp. 180–81.

18. Bohren, *Preaching and Community,* pp. 181–82.

19. Reuel Howe, *Partners in Preaching: Clergy and Laity in Dialogue* (New York: The Seabury Press, 1967), p. 47.

20. Achtemeier, *Creative Preaching,* p. 80.

21. "It happens frequently that the clergyman is confronted with a gathering that lacks the capacity to follow a connected discourse. The more the discourse approaches the form of a conversation, the more comprehensible the whole thing will be for such a gathering; therefore dialogue is the best form in such a situation." Friedrich Schleiermacher, *Praktische Theologie,* p. 304, as quoted in Bohren, *Preaching and Community,* p. 57.

22. Harry Emerson Fosdick, "What Is the Matter with Preaching?", *Pulpit Digest* 63 (September-October 1983): 12 [Reprint from *Harper's Magazine* 157 (July 1928)].

23. These basic suggestions are made in Brokhoff, "Preaching Dialogically," pp. 36–38.

24. Leonard J. Hatch, "Let Your Laymen Help You Preach," *The New Pulpit Digest* 57 (November-December 1977): 27.

25. Joseph Fort Newton, *The New Preaching* (Nashville: Cokesbury Press, 1930), pp. 120–24.

26. Thompson and Bennett, *Dialogue Preaching*, p. 9.

27. Fosdick alluded to an example of this kind of sermon form, calling it "an experiment in a new kind of preaching." Fosdick, "What Is the Matter?", p. 14.

28. Killinger, "The New Shape," p. 35.

29. Craddock, *Without Authority*, p. 55.

30. Achtemeier, *Creative Preaching*, p. 80.

31. For additional help with the dialogical sermon see George Swank, *Dialogic Style in Preaching*, The More Effective Preaching Series (Valley Forge, Pa.: Judson Press, 1981).

Part Four   The Narrative Message

1. G. Ernest Wright, *The God Who Acts: Biblical Theology as Recital* (London: SCM Press Ltd., 1952), p. 13.

2. Charles Rice, "The Preacher as Storyteller," *Union Seminary Quarterly Review* 31 (Spring, 1976): 188.

3. Don M. Wardlaw, ed., *Preaching Biblically* (Philadelphia: The Westminster Press, 1983), p. 11.

4. Augustine, *On Christian Doctrine*, 4. 2–3.

5. Henry H. Mitchell, *The Recovery of Preaching*, Harper's Ministers Paperback Library (San Francisco: Harper and Row, 1977), p. 75.

6. Amos N. Wilder, *The Language of the Gospel* (New York: Harper and Row, 1964), p. 10.

7. Edmund A. Steimle, Morris J. Niedenthal, and Charles R. Rice, *Preaching the Story* (Philadelphia: Fortress Press, 1980), p. 164.

8. See John Grossman, "You May Not Believe This One," *Geo* 5 (August 1983): 54.

9. Bibliography pertaining to Wiesel's books about biblical characters is provided in the earlier chapter on the "Dramatic Monologue Message." In addition to narratives about biblical characters, he has numerous other books of narratives on the market. For the concept of theology as narrative see *Interpretation* 37 (October 1983) [Most of the major articles focus on narrative and theology] and G. A. F. Knight, *Theology as Narration*:

A *Commentary on the Book of Exodus* (Grand Rapids: William B. Eerdmans Publishing Company, 1976). For communication as narrative see Howard Kambler, *Communication: Sharing Our Stories of Experience* (Seattle: Psychological Press, 1983).

10. Eugene L. Lowry, *The Homiletical Plot: The Sermon as Narrative Art Form* (Atlanta: John Knox Press, 1980), p. 88. Lowry advocates "a new image of the sermon" as "a narrative art form . . . akin to a play or novel" (p. 6), and much of the book is comprised of suggestions for structuring nonnarrative biblical literary genres into sermons with a "plot" structure. A helpful summary of Lowry's book can be found in Burton F. Blair, "Preaching as a Homiletical Plot," *Pulpit Digest* 62 (November-December, 1982): 23–25. See also Lowry, *Doing Time in the Pulpit: The Relationship Between Narrative and Preaching* (Nashville: Abingdon Press, 1985).

11. Steimle, Niedenthal, and Rice, *Preaching the Story,* p. 159.

12. The Academy of Homiletics, "Preaching and Story," p. 46. Compilation of papers presented to the annual meeting of the Academy of Homiletics, Princeton, New Jersey, 1979. (Mimeographed). The idea of using this text as an example comes from the source cited, but the suggestions for developing the sermon contain original concepts.

13. The idea of using this Scripture as an example came from Steimle, Niedenthal, and Rice, *Preaching the Story*, pp. 171–72. The suggested treatment of the text is my own.

14. Academy of Homiletics, "Preaching and Story," p. 45. The terminology is Wardlaw's.

15. Ibid. This suggestion was presented by Don Wardlaw.

16. Those wishing to explore this approach can look with profit at Frederick Buechner, *Telling the Truth: The Gospel As Tragedy, Comedy, and Fairy Tale.* (New York: Harper and Row, 1977).

17. For a helpful, succinct discussion of the relevance of redaction criticism, source criticism, and form criticism for preaching see William E. Hull, "Preaching on the Synoptic Gospels," pp. 169–94 in James W. Cox., ed. *Biblical Preaching: An Expositor's Treasury* (Philadelphia: The Westminster Press, 1983).

For individual volumes on the New Testament representative of original, European redaction criticism, which grew out of form critical perspectives, see Günther Bornkamm, Gerhard

Barth, and Heinz Joachim Held, *Tradition and Interpretation in Matthew*, trans. Percy Scott, in *The New Testament Library* (Philadelphia: The Westminster Press, 1963); Willi Marxsen, *Mark the Evangelist: Studies on the Redaction History of the Gospel*, trans. James Boyce, Donald Juel, William Poehlmann, with Roy A. Harrisville (Nashville: Abingdon Press, 1969); and Hanz Conzelmann, *The Theology of St. Luke*, trans. Geoffrey Buswell (New York: Harper and Brothers, 1960).

For individual volumes on the New Testament representative of redaction criticism from a more evangelical base see Robert Gundry, *Matthew, A Commentary on His Literary and Theological Art* (Grand Rapids: William B. Eerdmans Publishing Company, 1982); William Lane, *Commentary on the Gospel of Mark*, in *The New International Commentary on the New Testament* (Grand Rapids: William B. Eerdmans Publishing Company, 1974); Ralph Martin, *Mark, Evangelist and Theologian*, in *Contemporary Evangelical Perspectives* (Grand Rapids: Zondervan Publishing Corporation, 1972); and I. Howard Marshall, *Gospel of Luke: A Commentary on the Greek Text*, in *The New International Greek Testament Commentary* (Grand Rapids: William B. Eerdmans Publishing Company, 1978). An emerging series of commentaries offers promise of being helpful. See W. Ward Gasque, ed., *A Good News Commentary* (San Francisco: Harper and Row, various volumes available and forthcoming).

Similar concerns are evident in Old Testament studies. See Peter Ackroyd, James Barr, John Bright, and G. Ernest Wright, gen. eds., *The Old Testament Library* (Philadelphia: The Westminster Press, various volumes available and forthcoming).

Sets of commentaries on the entire Bible written from these perspectives are also in process. See Frank Moore Cross, Jr., and Helmut Koester, gen. eds., *Hermeneia—A Critical and Historical Commentary on the Whole Bible* (Philadelphia: Fortress Press, various volumes available and forthcoming). For a more evangelical approach see David A. Hubbard and Glenn W. Barker, gen. eds., *Word Biblical Commentary* (Waco, Tex.: Word Publishing Co., various volumes available and forthcoming.)

18. The currently developing method of biblical criticism called "structuralism" offers promise of additional help in dis-

covering the focus of a biblical narrative. Before it becomes helpful to most preachers, however, its theory and practice will have to be presented with conciseness and clarity. For a beginning at this see Daniel Patte, *What Is Structural Exegesis?* (Philadelphia: Fortress Press, 1976). You will find commentary help along these lines in the *Hermeneia* series and the *Word Biblical Commentary* series mentioned in the immediately preceding note.

A more detailed treatment will be found in a newly emerging series. See James Luther Mays, gen. ed., *Interpretation: A Biblical Commentary on Preaching and Teaching* (Atlanta: John Knox Press, various volumes available and forthcoming).

19. I am indebted to Lowry, *The Homiletical Plot*, pp. 89–95, for the scheme of organization for the following material and for some of the substance of the first three suggestions, although the material has been rearranged and substance added.

20. Ibid., p. 91.

21. Ibid.

22. Ibid., p. 92.

23. Ibid., pp. 90–91.

24. These three approaches and the quoted material explaining them appear in The Academy of Homiletics, "Preaching and Story," pp. 44–45.

25. Craddock, *Overhearing*, p. 137.

26. Steimle, Niedenthal, and Rice, *Preaching the Story*, p. 172.

27. Ibid.

28. Ibid.

29. Mitchell, *Recovery*, p. 90.

30. Richard A. Jensen, *Telling the Story* (Minneapolis: Augsburg Publishing House, 1980), pp. 146–47.

31. Mitchell, *Recovery*, p. 91.

32. Jensen, *Telling the Story*, pp. 134–35.

33. Ibid., p. 147.

34. Ibid., p. 145.

35. Academy of Homiletics, "Preaching and Story," pp. 23–24.

36. Richard Lischer, "The Limits of Story," *Interpretation* 38 (January 1984): 36. Lischer suggests "story" has its limits based on aesthetic, ontological, theological, and sociopolitical considerations.

37. Steimle, Niedenthal, and Rice, *Preaching the Story*, p. 166.

38. Ibid., p. 166

39. Ibid., p. 173.

40. Lowery, *Homiletical Plot*, p. 92.

41. Ibid., p. 94.

42. Craddock, *Overhearing*, p. 128.

43. Steimle, Niedenthal, and Rice, *Preaching the Story*, p. 13.

44. Ibid.

45. Ibid., p. 15.

46. Ibid., pp. 14–15.

47. Craddock, *Overhearing*, p. 123.

Part Five   Try Something Else

1. "The Coming Revolution in the World of Culture," A8.

2. Reid, *The Empty Pulpit*, p. 57.

3. Marshall McLuhan and Quentin Fiore, *The Medium Is the Massage* (New York: Random House, Inc., 1967), pp. 26, 63.

4. Michael Bell, "Preaching in Our Mass Media Environment," *Preaching* 4 (January-February 1969): 1.

5. Achtemeier, "The Artful Dialogue," p. 30.

6. Bettinghaus, *Persuasive Communication*, p. 168.

7. Emery Tang, "Understanding the Listener as a Movie-Goer," *Preaching* 2 (September-October 1967): 28.

8. Lyle Schaller, as quoted in "Growth Expert Cites Development," *The Baptist Standard* (June 15, 1977), p. 16.

9. Thor Hall, *The Future Shape of Preaching* (Philadelphia: Fortress Press, 1971), pp. 18, 128.

10. *Fort Worth Star-Telegram*, July 21, 1975.

11. Maynard Campbell, "An Investigation of the Incursion of Inductive Methodology into Preaching," (Ph.D. dissertation, Southwestern Baptist Theological Seminary, 1977), p. 277.

12. The suggested components are a synthesis of various specific suggestions made by Lloyd M. Perry, *Biblical Sermon Guide* (Grand Rapids: Baker Book House, 1970), pp. 53–54; Lloyd M. Perry, *Biblical Preaching for Today's World* (Chicago: Moody Press, 1973), pp. 116–24; Harold W. Ruopp, "Preaching to Life Situations," *Christian Century Pulpit* 6

(January 1935): 20; Harold Ruopp, "Life Situation Preaching," *Christian Century Pulpit* 12 (May 1941): 116; Ilion T. Jones, *Principles and Practices of Preaching* (New York: Abingdon Press, 1956), p. 107, n. 15, for a discussion of a five-step approach presented for discussion in 1955 at a meeting of the Association of Seminary Professors in the Practical Field.

13. Dwight E. Stevenson, In *The Biblical Preacher's Workshop* (Nashville: Abingdon Press, 1967), pp. 205–09.

14. For an extensive discussion of inductive preaching see Craddock, *As One Without Authority.* For additional help see Ralph L. Lewis with Gregg Lewis, *Inductive Preaching: Helping People Listen* (Westchester, Ill.: Crossway Books, 1983).

15. John Stacey, "Will Preaching Go On?" *Preacher's Quarterly* 15 (December 1969): 29.

16. For an example of a segmented sermon approach, see Elmer G. Homrighausen, "God's Story and Our Story," *Pulpit Digest* 60 (January-February 1980): 21–23.

17. William Jensen Reynolds, ed., *Hymns of Our Faith* (Nashville: Broadman Press, 1964).

18. John Stacey. "How Can a Local Preacher Experiment?" *Preacher's Quarterly* 15 (June 1969): 64.

19. Achtemeier, *Creative Preaching*, p. 77.

20. David E. Babin, "Examining the Potentialities of Monological Preaching," *Preaching* 5 (September-October 1970): 26.

Index

Acknowledgments

Permission to quote from the following sources is gratefully acknowledged:

Creative Preaching by Elizabeth Achtemeier. © 1980 by Abingdon Press.

An Introduction to Preaching by Daniel Baumann. © 1972. Published by Baker Book House.

Persuasive Communication by Erwin P. Bettinghaus. © 1973. Published by Holt, Rinehart and Winston. Reprinted by permission of CBS College Publishing.

Fundamentals of Speech Communication: The Credibility of Ideas by Bert E. Bradley. © 1974, 1978, 1981, 1984. Published by William C. Brown Publishers.

Between Man and Man by Martin Buber (Ronald Gregor Smith, trans.). © 1947. Published by Routledge and Kegan Paul, Ltd.

Overhearing the Gospel by Fred B. Craddock. © 1978 by Fred B. Craddock. Published by Abingdon Press.

The Renewal of Preaching by David James Randolph. © 1969. Published by Fortress Press.

The Future Shape of Preaching by Thor Hall. © 1971. Published by Fortress Press.

Preaching the Story by Edmund A. Steimle, Morris J. Niedenthal, and Charles R. Rice. © 1980. Published by Fortress Press.

"The Origins of the Sermon" by W. B. Sedgwick in *The Hibbert Journal* 45 (January 1947), courtesy of The Hibbert Trustees.

Communication and Persuasion by Carl I. Hovland, Irving L. Janis, and Harold H. Kelley. © 1953. Published by Yale University Press.

"The Artful Dialogue" by Elizabeth Achtemeier in *Interpretation* 35. © 1981. "The Limits of Story" by Richard Lischer in *Interpretation* 38. © 1984. Published by Union Theological Seminary in Virginia.

Telling the Story by Richard A. Jensen. © 1980. Published by Augsburg Publishing House.

"The New Shape of Preaching" by John Killinger in *Contemporary Christian Trends*, William M. Pinson and Clyde E. Fant, Jr., eds. © 1972. Published by Word Books.

Understanding the Media by Marshall McLuhan. © 1964. Published by McGraw-Hill Book Company.

"How Can the Local Preacher Experiment?" and "Will Preaching Go On?" by John Stacey in *The Preacher's Quarterly* (1969). Published by Epworth Press.

Dialogue Preaching by William D. Thompson and Gordon C. Bennett. © 1969. Published by Judson Press.

"The Coming Revolution in the World of Culture" in *U.S. News and World Report* (May 9, 1983). © 1983.

"Isaiah" in *The Broadman Bible Commentary*, Vol. 5. © 1971. Published by Broadman Press.

"Dogma Is Drama" by Alton McEachern in *Proclaim* 4. © 1974. Published by The Sunday School Board of the Southern Baptist Convention.

"Growth Expert Cites Development" in *The Baptist Standard* (June 15, 1977). © 1977.

HIEBERT LIBRARY

3 6877 00053 9501